W9-ADJ-649

My Connemara

Paula Steichen

New York

My Connemara

Harcourt, Brace & World, Inc.

These pages are dedicated to all that has been a part of Connemara—the fields and mountainland, the "million acres of sky," and the white house, the wild flowers, crops, trees, creatures and people. Especially the book is for my family—for the memory of my grandfather, for Gramma, Uncle Ed, John Carl, Marne and Janet, and for my mother, Helga, who so wisely set her children free to learn what they could from Connemara.

My deep appreciation goes to Helga for the continual support she gave me throughout the writing of this book and for the time and care she took in making editorial suggestions. Great thanks go also to her husband, Barney Crile, for his rare, generous way of showing enthusiasm and interest when it is most needed; and to my friend, Harvey Sloane, whose encouragement first prompted me to write this book. Lastly, I am very grateful to my grandmother and my noble, charming companion, Sinbad—my German shepherd dog—for their patient, unquestioning acceptance of the irregular hours and habits I adopt while writing.

Contents

My Connemara

KARLEN PAULA

I love thy face with a love given
to fresh flower blooms.
I love thy spoken words as the shimmer
of sun slants and the drift of rain.
If I should believe in angels and meet one
she would be somewhat like you.
Until I come to know one angel
worth cherishing I shall go on
in my cherishing of thy face and
spoken words.

—CARL SANDBURG
Connemara, 1946

We left the three-story Michigan house...

My family came from the Michigan dunelands. At least that is where they lived when I was born—and that is the part of the country most in the dreams of my mother. It was there that they first decided to have a Tom Thumb farm and raised a small dairy of milking goats. I was only a part of this for my first two years, and recall nothing of the tall house with scores of windows which had been designed by my grandmother, or the moving sands about us which were partially persuaded to stillness by my grandmother's planting of trees. How I wish I could remember those first hundreds of days! There are photos of my great-grandfather holding me in his careful, old arms. How can I not recall such arms? I was so young, I must have accepted all tributes with ease.

My freckle-faced brother, John Carl, who was a year and a half older than I, had spent his first year in a small farmhouse in O'Fallen, Illinois. Helga and my father were divorced, however, before I knew his voice or face. She had returned with the baby boy to her parents' Michigan home at Harbert shortly before I was born. So it was there that I took my first

5

steps and inspected a bowl of goldfish for the first time, crying when the adults at last led me from the sight. I learned to speak, calling my mother "Helga," my grandparents "Gramma" and "Buppong," and my two aunts "Marne" and "Janet."

Twenty years later my mother and I travelled back to that house and that land to visit the lake once again. I saw the porch where my great-grandfather and I had posed for the photographer and there was something in the scent and the winding of the paths that stirred me, but I did not truly remember.

In 1945 the newspapers ran a picture of my grandfather reading a story backwards to John Carl and me with the caption, "Coming Down South—Harbert, Mich., Nov. 10—Carl Sandburg, famed Lincoln biographer and poet, reads to his two grandchildren, Karlen Paula and John Carl, in his home on the Lake Michigan sand dunes here. He is leaving to live on a newly acquired estate at Hendersonville, N.C."

One paper quoted the head of the house as saying, "A long time ago I told her [Mrs. Sandburg] and my daughter Helga that whenever and wherever they found a place they liked better than Harbert, Michigan, we'd pull up roots. So—we're pulling them up." And a Chicago paper speculated, "For Carl Sandburg the move to North Carolina will be a hard pull. It has been made necessary, we learn, by the icy winds that sweep the Michigan sand dunes in winter. Mr. Sandburg has acquired a historic estate in which he can commune with ghosts of the Civil War. It is the house of Christopher Memminger, secretary of the Confederate treasury under Jefferson Davis, near Hendersonville, N.C."

This grand "estate," to which the newspapers referred, in actuality became a working farm under the hands of Helga and Gramma. It had become essential for the Sandburg family to have a large home after my grandfather's writing career was under way. Not only did he have twelve thousand books which had to be placed on shelves where they could be selected as needed, but our way of living also demanded enough space so that he could work and rest undisturbed by the activities of his energetic family.

My grandmother had first passed through this mountain region in the late thirties on a vacation leading her to Florida and back to the Great Lakes. During her visit in Asheville she had exclaimed, "The air is somehow different here!" Years later, when the family decided to go in search of a farm where the goats could be raised in the manner of a real dairy, they turned to the western North Carolina mountains that were so well remembered—where the grass remained green ten months out of the year. In 1945 Helga, Gramma and my grandmother's sister-in-law, Dana Steichen, set out to find the right home for the Sandburg family. When they reached Asheville, the real-estate man gave them three choices of farms. "Connemara," in Flat Rock about twenty-five miles south of Asheville, was the one place where the barn was far enough from the house so that none of the clatter of milk pails or excited calls to stray cows or pigs would carry to the writer's working quarters. Beyond the great field rolling downhill to a lake at the front of the house one could see the Smoky Mountains—and rising at the rear of the house was the hazy Blue Ridge range.

Gramma always declared that she bought Connemara because of the winding driveway banked with one-hundred-foot pine trees and an ivy-covered stone wall. For Helga, the decision was made when she sighted the sloping fields and spreading oak limbs under which the goats could graze and rest content in summer sun. For my grandfather the matter was decided when he stepped onto the front porch and looked

Paula, Buppong and John Carl in Harbert, Michigan, 1945, just before moving to Connemara.

Three people, nice people, the one in the middle not so sweet fine nice as the two on the ends but the three of them rather elegant and thoughtful = To which we sign our names without swearing to it =

Buppong
JOHN CARL
PAULA

(Sept 11-47)

Buppong wrote his own caption for the photo a few years later

past pillars to the distant dusky-blue hills. He put his hand on the porch railing and declared that Connemara would be the new home. He then chose two small loftlike rooms with western exposure for his own. Here in the years to come he would work undisturbed, often retiring to his bed just as the farmers in the family were rising below, putting coffee on the stove and calling the dogs to go with them to the early milking. Sometimes the writer would call or wave from his high windows as one struck out into the dark morning—the moon low and mellowed, giving the one hint of the dawn to come. He would enjoy this waking of farm life as he was turning to sleep. "You look like you know where you're going," he would call out. "If you get lost I bet you'll follow the stars!"

It was my grandmother, along with Aunt Janet and a helper, Adeline Polega, who went to Connemara after the purchase to command the carpenters and electricians. Helga remained in Harbert with us children and Marne and Buppong —caring for the animals, packing and preparing for the move. Connemara was an outdated home that required many changes. There were only two bathrooms in this house of some thirty or more rooms, yet there were washbasins in almost all the rooms, and two in the master bedroom. The caretaker's son shook his head and suggested the reason for the double basins: "I guess one was for him and one for her!"

The ceilings were too high to permit proper heating and there was no kitchen in the main house. As in many Civil War homes, there was a separate building for cooking and another for laundry. My grandfather often said, "We didn't buy a farm when we bought Connemara, we bought a small village." There were eleven buildings along her twisting paths and driveways. Many of them were converted for farm use. Less expansive than former owners, Gramma had a kitchen built in the house and converted the old one into a three-car garage. The laundry house, with its great round concrete tubs, became the chicken house, and eventually we kept the first-born kids there in springtime. One spacious house with decorated eaves and a steeply sloping roof was dubbed the "Swedish House" and soon held the overflow library and old magazines. Another structure was changed to serve as a cheese house, which in summer months would hold a heavy scent of the anise and caraway my mother mixed into her soft, aging goat cheeses; and one of the buck houses, where the prize beasts would chew their grain in peace, had once been the washerwoman's establishment. The elaborate fountain on the front lawn was dismantled and became instead a quiet pool where John Carl and I would spend many hours sailing boats or cooling our bare feet. There were sinks and bathtubs and cabinets to install in the main house, walls to be repainted, furniture and livestock to be received and cared for.

My grandmother and mother exchanged letters in the excitement of moving. "Dear Carl and Helga and babes—All is coming along fine here—a little slow but coming surely. We are very comfortable in a few rooms that are finished. . . . You are more comfortable up there with the children—at least for another two weeks, on account of the painting and carpentry and dirt from the plaster.

"The house heats very well I am sure—but with the workmen around leaving doors open, it would not be so good for the children.

"We had a long walk up the mountains Sunday—Ballard (the caretaker) going with us so we wouldn't get lost! We found that our land goes up over the top of Little Glassy Mountain and up to the very top of Big Glassy Mountain—at least a mile of real climbing from the house. The timber seems endless—mostly oak, black gum, yellow pine, white pine, hickory—with dogwood everywhere. The hills will be white with dogwood blossoms in spring. There are many trails and paths through the mountains—perfect for horseback riding.

"We walked up and down the mountain for three hours Sunday—a perfect day—air crisp and winey! How Dad will enjoy these walks! From the top of Big Glassy you see all over Hendersonville and the country all about, Smokies and Blue Ridge—a far wider view than from our porch—and in every direction as you are 'on top of the World!' "

My mother wrote of practical matters: "The goats left this morning, 22 instead of 18, as there seemed to be room to spare. . . . The Farmer's Exchange will take the straw that is left, at $15 per ton, and I'm getting the hay out of the way too, either thru them or a farmer they send. . . . The weather has turned very cold and damp. I am glad the goats are gone. . . ."

There were farm articles to inquire about: "Don't forget the wheelbarrow and all the good garden hose. . . . There is a small roll of new fencing by the buck house. Be sure to bring that." And all the familiar objects: "Shall I send the crockery? I mean the big stone crocks for pickles, sauerkraut, wine, etc.?" And Gramma, skeptical of newness, worried, "Be sure to take down the good can opener on the wall. You can't buy a good one. So better pack it now before you forget."

It was wartime when we moved from Michigan—fall of 1945. "Adeline says that she told you that she would take the Ration Books—but that she forgot and did not bring any. Be sure to bring all our sugar. The sugar stamps are all that is needed now." Then Gramma's letters always turned once more to the new land: "There are many wild enchanting spots—with steep cliffs impossible to climb, except by going around. We found blueberry stands. . . . I am more than ever impressed with the great extent of the tract and the many

spots with glorious views of distant mountains and perpendicu-
lar cliffs of glassy rock. It is Wilderness indeed!"

This wilderness and the old white house with gun turrets
and great fluted columns and newly painted walls—with dairy-
lands, barns and fields—this was the new world where I would
grow up, exploring foot by foot and day by day for a decade
every stream, branch and cavern, most often with my brother
and Buppong.

This wilderness of Connemara, this wild, sweet way of
Connemara, would come back to me always after leaving—in
the scent of wild blackberries, the nickering of a colt watching
its mother being led away to plow, the feel of wet morning
grass on bare feet, and the moving of a herd at milking time
up the pasture lane—a little hurried, anticipating the sweet
molasses grain and the company of the herdsmen and my
mother, caring for and coaxing them, considerate and firm.

"Buppong comes down this morning, I am working, Mom is writing, Janet is doing dishes, Margaret is dusting, Little Paus'l orders him to stand up and then sit down and then stand up again. 'What a house!' he said. 'Women managing everything. Ed should see this. Little John and I, we've got to put up some front!' Buppong is a dear—"

—HELGA SANDBURG
Journal, 1946

June Glenn, Jr. (Asheville *Citizen Times*)

Buppong

The family that moved into the big house...

The family that moved into the big house at Connemara consisted of seven members—as varied as any people could possi-
bly have been. Being the only man in our household, my
grandfather was naturally the head of this family which was
made up of his wife, three daughters and two grandchildren.
But though he took delight in all the farm activities that he
saw about him, or which the family related to him, he never,
in any sense, commanded the farm operations. He left almost
all the practical, day-to-day decisions to his wife and daughters. Gramma had handled the finances in the family since she
and Buppong were married, and now she shared with Helga
the responsibility of running the household and the farm—
hiring the workers, planning the breeding of the goats, the
planting of trees and fields, and the building of fences.

When an old oak near the house had to be cut down and
hauled away, it was Gramma and Helga who oversaw the
workers—reasoning with the puzzled men, telling them to
"Fell it in that direction—to hit the wall and not these old
boxwoods!" The men found it hard to understand why anyone

would prefer to knock down a wall which would have to be rebuilt, rather than crush a small section of the aged evergreens.

Soon after settling in at Connemara, Helga selected a spot to hoist the huge bell that had rung across the sand dunes in Michigan each time one of the girls had to be called to the house from the lake or the barn. At Connemara the bell was set on a tall cedar post across from the chicken house. A code of rings was established: one pull of the long rope would call the caretaker, two would be for Janet, three would be for John Carl and myself, and continual ringing would mean that everyone must assemble for some emergency.

Connemara soon became home. In the living room, two thick books could be seen piled one on the other near a straight-backed chair, where my grandfather would prop his left foot as he played the guitar in the evenings. Later, two Sears, Roebuck catalogs would often replace the books. The collection of canes given to Buppong by friends was set about the house: in corners of rooms, by the fireplace, in wastebaskets, huge crocks and cardboard boxes. And an assortment of felt hats soon rested on the table near the front door along with a sweater or two and several scarves for Buppong to choose from as he went out walking, draping the sweater about his shoulders in chilly weather, a scarf knotted around his neck.

In a far corner of the living room, a small walnut and glass cabinet was placed behind the grand piano. Over the years John Carl and I would go to this cabinet infrequently and sit on the piano bench nearby as we studied its contents, absorbed in the treasures we found there. Its three shelves held in disorder dozens of cases and paper boxes, some as large as our hands, some as small as our thumbs. Lifting the cover of one we might see a ring made out of a dollar bill, a miniature guitar, some Swedish coins, an Indian head penny, a coin celebrating the third inauguration of FDR and a "Reward of Merit" given to Lilie M. Steichen when she was in grade school. Lying free on the shelves were large round skipping stones from Lake Michigan. Amongst them we would find a Pulitzer Prize, a Pegasus award or the North Star medal—heavy objects shining, some bronze, some silver, some gold, a few of heavy steel—and often they had brilliant ribbons attached—scarlets, golds, deep blues and vivid greens—we traced them, satin, with our fingers.

As intriguing as the shining awards was a polished skull of a small animal, ivory and perfect, and crumpled envelopes containing dusty bullets from another age. On one such envelope my grandfather had written "Appomattox," and we

Paula, Helga and John Carl

children grew to know a quiet fear as we learned to read and to recognize the name. At a younger age we appreciated more the blue box filled with hand-decorated sugar cubes, the set of Lincoln pennies someone had sent to Buppong, and the minute figure of a goat made of metal. The only objects in the cabinet we considered lacking in interest were the scrolls of paper on the bottom shelves—degrees, certificates, awards—rolled tight and tied with dark scholarly ribbons. Our beacon to this store of treasures was a familiar framed piece of writing which always sat on the top of the cabinet. Even before I knew the alphabet, I liked the odd design of the writing. One day I finally read the words: "Will Mr. Rodney do Th. Jefferson the favor to take family soup with him tomorrow? Jan 24, '09."

Throughout the house, John and I watched the library being put into place. Both Margaret and Gramma tried to organize the books in terms of subject matter. Marne made continual efforts over the years to keep the poetry in the dining room, the history in the utility room, the social reform books in a front room, and so on. But Buppong had his own organization. He would pass the shelves and casually bring down a book, remarking, "I just might need this book. I think I'll take it upstairs with me," or, eyeing a title high on some shelf, he would decide, "That book doesn't deserve to be with the others!" and relegate it to a stack exiled to the Swedish House.

The family quickly formed the habit of spending much time out of doors at Connemara, each member choosing his own hours to walk about the fields and mountainsides. When Gramma was not at her desk in the Farm Office, we usually could find her checking the progress of her gardens around the house, or at the barn conferring with Helga. She took frequent walks, bending often on her way to clear pine cones or sticks from the path and always picking up any bits of paper she might find.

Gramma

Janet and Helga were the earliest risers in the family, waking before dawn to leave their warm beds and tend the animals. Margaret, in contrast, sometimes went to sleep just as they were rising, following the habits of her father. She and Buppong shared the custom of walking at night, too. In the early evening the whole family might go together past the tall pines of the front drive, circling into the side pasture before returning to the house; but it was Marne and Buppong who often walked in the dark, alone or together, after the rest of the house was quiet. When I grew older I sometimes slept at the top of the house in the "crow's nest." On a moonless night I could see the glow of their flashlight dancing slowly down the drive, pausing at the call of a night bird, and sometimes I would hear them singing softly as they returned from such a walk:

> *When other lips and other hearts*
> *Their tales of love shall tell*
> *In language whose excess imparts*
> *The power they feel so well*
> *There may perhaps in such a scene*
> *Some recollection be*
> *Of days that have as happy been*
> *Then you'll remember me.*

If there was ever a reason to fear the night at Connemara, the family seemed oblivious of it. The house was never locked and the keys were always left in the car. Margaret sometimes went alone in the deep of night to swim in the waters of the side lake, as she had done in Lake Michigan years before. Her figure, small and slightly stooped in the vague light of moon and stars, moved slowly, quietly—without hurry or fear.

She was the eldest of the daughters, five years older than Janet. At the age of nine she had been found to have nocturnal epilepsy. Specialists were consulted and several cures were attempted, one involving complete fasting for long periods, another a strict control of the diet. These violent treatments combined with the experimental drugs did not help Margaret's health, already weakened by the seizures. She remained in good spirits, however, cooperative through it all—having an affectionate nature and being close to her mother and sisters. Because she was never able to regain the vigor that she had had as a very young child, her life usually revolved around Connemara's library and her own intellectual pursuits rather than the farming activities.

Marne with her dog Shawn and John Carl

Though Marne never completed school because of her illness, she managed to do an impressive job of educating herself throughout the years. A voracious reader, she is the only person I have ever known who can recall and relate the plot of almost any classical novel, and who has read and marked the *Encyclopaedia Britannica* from A to Z.

She has always had an extreme gentleness with children and animals. My mother recalls an incident in Michigan when she returned from college to find her Great Dane pup, Jon, grown huge, and since he had had no training while she had been away, quite unpredictable. The family was sitting at the dinner table, and some abrupt movement from Margaret caused Jon to snarl and leap at her, lacerating her arm. As Helga ran forward to punish the dog, she could hear her sister's cry, "Don't hit Jon. He didn't know what he was doing—I shouldn't have moved so suddenly."

Marne played our grand piano and tried valiantly to teach her young niece and nephew to play also. She was patient and encouraging when we arrived for our individual lessons in the front room. She praised us when we showed any signs of mastering our stubborn fingers, and even arranged brief recitals for her pupils, the family duly assembling at the designated hour to watch us work studiously over the keyboard, trying to hold in our heads the hours of kind instruction and the hateful rhythm of the metronome. At last the lessons were abandoned, the grownups unsure of the decision, we children bursting out the door and down the steps to return to our reckless play. My fingers, so clumsy an hour before, suddenly regained their usefulness as they entangled themselves in the horses' manes or pulled up the ladder into the dark, secret parts of the haylofts.

Our Aunt Margaret was briefly disappointed in the failure of the lessons, but she soon became absorbed again in her studies of history and researching of facts and lines for songs. She was as thorough and precise in her scholarly pursuits as Janet was reliable in the feeding of the kids or informing one of the weather forecast.

Along with Helga, my Aunt Janet helped with the farm work, rising every morning at 5:30 to feed the dogs and give the first milk-feeding to the baby goats. She took charge of all the kids which arrived in singles, twins, triplets and often quadruplets from Christmastime until June. Several times a day she measured heated milk into double rows of white pans, then let the mob of kids loose to hurtle down the runway and push their heads into the stanchions. They drank with loud sucking noises, butting the pans passionately when the last bit of milk was gone. The kids had been taken away from their mothers when they were just a few minutes old, and they rightly considered Janet the one who cared for them. When they caught sight of her opening the long barnyard gate, they would begin to bleat eagerly, anticipating the grain and milk which she would soon produce for them.

Finished with her early chores, Janet would return to the house and to the well-ordered schedule she had set for herself. She helped with the housework and had her own interests— reading or drawing in her room on the top floor. She was the middle daughter, two and a half years older than Helga. When she was young, Janet had been hit by a car, suffering severe headaches for many years after the accident. She always remained at home, and gradually she seemed to adopt the simpler and happier qualities of all the world around her. Buppong and Gramma never expected more from her than she was able to accomplish, and their acceptance of her abilities no doubt had a great deal to do with her contentment. In her sunny, impulsive way Janet befriended most of the people she met on the bus or in town. Travelling back into the mountains, I often heard the refrain, "Oh, I know your Aunt Janet. Tell her to come and visit us sometime. We'd really enjoy that!"

Janet with her cat Kitty Whispers

We children were at ease with Janet, sensing that she was more like us than the adults. While we regarded Marne with the respect due an aunt, we generally viewed Janet with a more comradely, competitive air. The three of us had distinct favorites in almost every subject we could think of—colors, animals, flowers, heroes. Staunchly faithful to Gene Autry and Champion, I would note Janet's pictures of Roy Rogers and Trigger with appropriate disdain when I went visiting in her long room. She taped her pictures to closet doors—alongside Roy Rogers were myriad pictures of cats, and one of a young and innocent-looking Elizabeth Taylor, a suave Cary Grant, and at least one photo of the current Democratic favorite or President.

Her room was usually in a state of activity and slight confusion, filled with knickknacks and Janet's current projects—cutting nature photos from a stack of magazines or assembling a scrapbook on historic sights. So different from Margaret's room, which was filled with art pieces from foreign lands and books on painting and ancient history, Janet's room had its personal flavor and the rest of the family usually did not interfere with it. Only occasionally, when Janet was away visiting, Helga would march to her sister's room and fill boxes with what she considered would not be missed, and would burn them. She would dust and set the room in order, and when Janet returned from her trip, she would compliment her sister's work. Then gradually the room would return to its accustomed and comforting disarray.

From a card table near her bed, Janet continually carried on correspondence with people met throughout a lifetime. When I was away from Connemara, I looked forward to Janet's letters, always full of the information I wanted most to hear: "Bebe had four kids. The pink dogwood are blooming. The purple finches are still here. It is warm outside. How is it where you are?" Her traditional signature was, "I think of you quite often. Loads of love, Janet."

Every morning of my grandfather's life at Connemara—until almost the end, Janet brought a breakfast tray to his door, which would be picked up at an hour that reflected how late the writer had worked into the night. On the tray she placed a piece of cheese, a slice of rye or pumpernickel bread, a glass of goat milk, a thermos of coffee, a jar of honey and some seasonal fruit. Sometimes this would keep her father until the evening meal if he was immersed in work or reading.

Buppong had a gentle way with Janet. He called her "Jannie" often and always had a bit of praise for her "bright waist," or her way with the animals, or her grey-blue Steichen eyes. Hearing her cry out as she overturned a hot thermos of coffee one morning while mounting the stairs to his bedroom, Buppong rushed from his sleep to soothe her on the stairway. "It's all right, Jannie, it's all right. . . . We'll put some salve on your arm. . . . The breakfast doesn't matter. . . ." And listening to her strong voice echoing over Connemara when she called the kids from pasture or announced that dinner was ready, he would often laugh and declare, "She missed her calling as an opera star!"

This was the family then: the grandparents—Buppong and Gramma; the three daughters—Margaret, with her gentle, quiet mannerisms, Janet, with her sure and energetic way of speaking and going from room to room, and Helga; and Helga's children—John Carl and I. The scope in age, worldliness, intellect, strength and interests was immense, and formed at Connemara a world within itself, a world often seeming to have infinite range and possibility.

"Chikaming—a great name in goats!"

> —*The Goat World*
> May, 1947

"The Chikaming Herd of dairy goats were moved down from our farm in Michigan about 18 months ago. We are finally settled here in Henderson County and cannot praise this country highly enough. . . ."

> ——HELGA SANDBURG
> *Farmer's Federation News*
> August, 1947

Part of the Chikaming herd on pasture, below the barn at Connemara

The goats...

At the foot of Connemara's two mountains, Big and Little Glassy, lay the forty-odd acres of pastureland which held the family's goats each sunny day. In the morning, directly after milking, the barn doors and the gates to the pasture would be opened, and the goats would head down into the fields of mixed clover and alfalfa and lespedeza; as evening approached, they would be crowding at the gate of the pasture eager to be let back up the lane to the night milking. Unlike many goat breeders who feed their animals in paddocks throughout the year, Gramma and Helga considered this open grazing important for the goats' welfare, providing them with exercise and a choice of roughage and grasses.

All of the pastures at Connemara were fed by spring brooks coming from the mountainsides. Along the glint of water, and in scattered groups throughout the fields, grew spreading oaks and pines under which the goats would gather in the heat of day, kneeling on the soft bed of pine needles and oak leaves left from falltime, groaning occasionally in their gentle expression of contentment.

At any time, under the trees or spread over the green of the fields, they created a picture full of color, for their coats ranged from a pure white to red, black and all shades of brown. Our dairy was stocked with three breeds: two Swiss breeds with pricked ears—the white Saanans, and the Toggenburgs with their regular markings of white trim on brown coats; and the Nubians, whose ancestors were imported from England as Anglo-Nubians—the result of crossing African bucks that had been presented to the Queen, with English goats. The Nubian ears were pendulous and delicately turned at the ends, and they were sometimes silvered; their coats varied— in mottled, splashed or solid colors. Each breed had its place in our dairy, the Saanans and Toggenburgs giving a greater amount of milk than the Nubians, but having less butterfat than the Nubian milk with its exceptional flavor.

All of our older does were on Advanced Registry Test— the recognized method of testing milk production. One evening each month an official state tester would arrive unannounced to preside over the milking and see that the udders of all the animals on test were stripped clean. Then he would supervise the morning and evening milking the next day, weighing the milk and determining the butterfat content. In this way the goats who gave excellent performances could be recognized by goat breeders throughout the country, and kids could then be purchased on the basis of the production of their dams, daughters, sisters and various relatives. Connemara became well known as a dairy farm and Gramma as a top goat breeder—the stock always in demand, kids, bucks, bred does, and the stud service of the bucks. Many times I was to hear a visiting goat enthusiast remark, "You mean her husband is the *same* Carl Sandburg?"

Gramma and Helga managed the herd together, each one keeping in touch with all aspects, but with Gramma essentially

Farmer's Federation News

John holding a Toggenburg kid, Paula with a Nubian. Note the disbudding scars on the Nubian's head

directing the breeding and Helga handling the management side of the business. Much of my grandmother's work was done at her desk in the Farm Office, studying the pedigrees and production records of each goat and its relatives. She was fascinated by the complicated study of genetics in breeding and read everything on the subject. Gramma aimed for high production and show type in the Chikaming herd, and in order to attain this she had to be fully familiar with each goat's record, pedigree and progeny.

Now and then Gramma would pack her bag and put on the hat she wore for travelling or going to town and be off to lecture some goat breeders at one of their annual meetings. My mother used to tell John Carl and me how once in Michigan before we were born there was a severe blizzard at the time of one of the American Milk Goat Record Association meetings. Helga had saddled two horses then, putting the Western saddle on one for Gramma, and, carrying the suitcase on hers, they had ridden through the drifts the mile out to the highway to catch a bus.

My brother and I were accustomed to seeing Gramma at her desk a great deal of the time, her head bent over the records of dams, sires and daughters, studying pedigrees, proposed matings, and the percentage of inbreeding. At a time when I knew nothing of genetics, I greatly admired Gramma's familiarity with each goat in the herd. She could discuss the lineage of the goats for hours with the family or her friends, calling each goat by name and citing its parents, siblings and daughters. The names for the kids were chosen with care as they were born, with a mind toward their inheritance. The does of each family of goats had names beginning with the same letter. Thus, two of Gloria's daughters were Glory and Ginevra, and Ginevra's daughters were Guinevere, Giovana and Gentian; and in another fine Toggenburg family Blyth

Gramma with her favorite Nubian doe, Brocade

gave birth to Bluebell, and Bluebell in time gave birth to Bluebird and Britt and Brio, and then Bluebird's daughters were
Blueberry and Bluebonnet, Brielle and Brigitte. The culmina-
tion of all the years of planned inbreeding with Toggenburgs
came in 1961 when Gramma's doe, Puritan Jon's Jennifer II,
became the all-breed American champion in milk production,
and the world-wide Toggenburg champion. The doe, weighing
170 pounds, produced 5,750 pounds of milk and 191 pounds
of butterfat in 305 days.

Since Gramma was less intent on line-breeding the Nubians,
we eventually dropped the custom of naming them in terms of
first letters, and named them instead for their temperament

Paula with Toggenburg kids

or appearance. The delicate patterns of the Nubian coats
prompted such titles as Batiste, Brocade, Fern, Cameo, Opal,
Amber, Topaz, Jewel, Onyx, Mauve. The kids, who were
taken from their mothers at birth, were raised together in
separate quarters. I spent many hours on the grassy slope that
was theirs, playing with them, watching them race toward
me in a sunny, frolicking group as I called out their names,
which sometimes spoke of the passing of time: Midnight,
Dawn, Morn; and sometimes of the flowers on Connemara's
mountain paths, her fields and summer garden: Bluet, Butter-
cup, Primrose, Pansy, Briarrose, Jasmine, Dewrose, Poppy.

In the area outside the "kid quarters" Helga set barrels and
wooden planks on which the kids could play. Energetic, they
would leap onto the oil drums and dance on their hind legs,
pirouetting into the air to come down on stiff legs, making
short hops back to the ground, their heads cocked to one side,
the long ears of the Nubians flying. As the family watched
them, admiring, more names would be decided upon: Balle-
rina, Citation, Bravo, Twink, Fiesta, Fan-Fair, Ballet.

During the years when we were living at Connemara and
Helga was managing the dairy, she rose early each morning
to work with the herdsmen in the milking of the nine or ten
strings of goats—six does standing on the milking platform at
a time. A radio played country and popular music during those
early hours—and there were heaters to take the chill out of the
rooms in the winter months. Some days I would follow Helga
in the dawn, taking with me a bowl of cereal which she would
fill for me with newly drawn goat milk. I ate my breakfast
perched high on sacks of grain as "I'm Looking Over a Four
Leaf Clover" or "You Are My Sunshine" came out of the
radio mingled with static. The ancient machine had its cord
mended here and there with old-fashioned adhesive tape—wide
and heavy—which Helga would bring down from the first-aid

cabinet when needed, feeling that it did as good a job as black, electrician's tape could do. There was always a litter of yellow kittens in the hayloft or among the grain sacks, who would soon grow old enough to join the circle of eager cats who thrust their whiskers deep through the foam of the warm milk that was placed before them.

In the milking room, the white-uniformed workers moved purposefully about me as I sat playing with the kittens on the cool concrete floor. Occasionally I begged to be allowed to milk a favorite goat, and a worker, amused and patient, would set me on one of the six cement arcs where those who were milking the goats stood at the high platform. As I grew, I measured myself in comparison to this platform—one day finding that I could just look over its ledge, and another morning fitting my elbows over the top and hoisting myself up. No matter what height I was, I could always run up the cement steps, as the milking does did, and thrust my head through the stanchions to the smell of the sweet-feed in the buckets there.

How I wished I were a goat at times! One bin in the grain room held the citrus pulp—dried peelings of oranges and grapefruits and lemons—the smell a blend of honeyed ripe fruits and dusky haylofts. Against orders I would climb into the bin and bring the wooden lid down over the top till all was musk and dark, and chewing on a hard slip of lemon I would dwell on the loveliness of being an animal. I felt I understood the dark and secret parts of their nature and the ways of their world.

There was also a bin of whole kernel corn that gave way when you crawled in, allowing toes and ankles and legs to work down under the hard golden kernels so smooth to touch. The third and last bin was filled with sweet-feed made of oats and cracked corn, bran and molasses, which stuck to your feet and was not so good to play in, but which could be chewed until all the molasses was gone and then spit out onto the ground.

During the months when the does were freshening, a keg of molasses was kept in the feed room along with a container of salt and a bag of bran. As Helga knelt in the straw by the anxious doe, reassuring her and, if necessary, helping her bring forth the babies with their sprawling legs and coating of caul, someone would heat a pan of hot water on the stove. When the kids were delivered, a helper would rush them out of the mother's sight and up to the house for attention and warmth, while Helga let the dam lick her hands and hair as if she were its kid, and talked quietly to her, feeding her a steaming bucket of bran, molasses and salt. I would fill my cupped hands with the delicious mixture just as it was set down, feeling how satisfied the doe must be, and when we left the barn, we could look back to see the goat still busily eating the sweet bran from her bucket.

My carrot-haired brother, John Carl, and I played for long hours in the barn, often stopping to watch or help with the many tasks: the shearing of coats for summertime, the tattooing, worming, weighing, feeding. When Helga trimmed the goats' hoofs, we sometimes helped her catch the more flighty does, and we often climbed to the dusky loft to push down bales of hay for the caretaker to spread in the racks below. Following our mother as she attended to the chores—quick and competent—or checked on her workers, we children grew accustomed to all the farm sights, from the butchering of the pigs to the plowing of the fields.

John Carl and I were rarely sheltered from any of the farm activities, and it was our duty as well as everyone else's to notice when a doe came into heat. The bucks were purposely kept in a field bordering the lane that the does followed as they returned from pasture. Those that were in heat would linger by the fence line, wagging their tails and accepting the enthusiastic appreciation of the bucks crowding the fence nearby. Helga would consult the breeding chart, tacked up early in the season, to be certain that each doe was serviced by the proper buck, and then the goat would be led back to the lane and bred.

Since most does come into heat in late summer, fall and winter, sometimes a heat would be skipped or encouraged earlier in the year by penning selected does with a buck for a month or so, in order that all of the milkers would not freshen at the same time. This provided the dairy with milk the year round.

Each morning and evening the milk was strained into three-gallon cans in the milking room, and when one was full it was carried into the grey, concrete-block milk house, cooled over cold-water pipes, and then put in huge steel coolers. Handled in sterilized containers throughout the process, the milk was taken every morning to the Kalmia Dairy in nearby Hendersonville, where it was sold in single-use paper containers throughout the southeast. I often went along for the ride to the dairy and would sit on the loading ramp with John Carl, our feet dangling—drinking chocolate milk through a straw in the pint cartons that Helga bought for us before she went in to attend to her business.

The Chikaming herd usually sold all the milk it could produce. There was a steady demand for it for babies or ill and elderly people who could not digest cow's milk. I frequently heard Gramma explaining to dubious visitors that goat's milk is naturally homogenized and alkaline in reaction, unlike that of a cow, and this is the reason that it takes only twenty minutes for digestion, whereas cow's milk takes two hours. Of course John Carl and I loved goat's milk and thought that almost everybody drank it. We would echo Buppong's claim, "If it tastes any different from cow's milk, goat's milk tastes better!"

When there was surplus milk Helga and Gramma sometimes made cheeses. Helga liked best to make the Brie types, plain or seasoned with anise or caraway seeds, while Gramma specialized in Neufchâtels. Both women made a smooth, caramel-colored cheese with such a strong scent at times that it caused John and me to circle clear of the containers, wrinkling up our faces as we did so. The cheese house was an intriguing place to us children—dimly lighted, filled with the two women's crocks and coffee cans covered with cloth, and with the strong acid scent of the aging cheeses. We watched the food being smoothed with wide wooden paddles there, as the liquid was drawn off for the dogs; and after nine days or more of curing, we would help carry the cheeses to the kitchen to be paraffined or transferred to cold storage.

In addition to cheeses, the family made buttermilk, butter, and yogurt which would sit a whole afternoon among the potted plants in the sun of the kitchen windows wrapped in bright towels. My favorite of all these dairy products, however, was the goat cream. A separator had to be used since the milk is naturally homogenized, and through repeated separation the cream could be made as thick as soft butter. It was pure white and without the heaviness of cow's cream. John and I ate quantities of it mixed with sugar and fresh berries or cereal.

The entire family was charmed by the goats—the playful acrobatics of the kids and the gentle, friendly way of the milking does. Buppong often encouraged us to bring a kid to him on the front porch or front lawn where it would put on a show for the whole family. And we sometimes brought them into the living room after lunch, to play and explore the people and furniture. Any misbehaving was simply mopped or picked up from the rug—and the show continued.

The older does were just as curious and affectionate as the kids, if not so active. My grandmother would walk about the barn discussing matters with Helga, an entourage of does following the two women, chewing intently on the hems of Gramma's dresses, already repaired carefully from previous attentions, and nibbling the buttons of coats, blowing softly into our faces and nuzzling our necks if we bent over or sat on the stone wall in the barnyard.

The does loved attention and responded accordingly. Handled constantly and kept in clean quarters and away from the males, which are often almost odorless in the Nubian breed in summer, but are rank in the Swiss breeds all year long, they had none of the strong odor or aggressiveness goats are sometimes noted for, smelling only slightly of fragrant hay and of field grass in summer. Around their necks each had a leather collar which Helga had tooled with the doe's name. Some special pets knew to look for cigarettes in the herdsman's shirt pocket, enjoying tobacco just as they relished the pine boughs and honeysuckle that Gramma would often bring to them, and the fresh parings of apples from the day's baking, and the orange peelings and grapefruit rinds brought from the breakfast table.

There was only one aspect of dairy farming to which I never became resigned. Soon after the birth of each kid, Helga determined whether or not the goat would have horns. Some were born naturally hornless; those that were not had to be "disbudded" a few days after birth, disbudding being the only practical way of keeping a hornless herd. Many problems developed if a kid was allowed to grow horns. Though goats are naturally gentle animals, they shove one another occasionally as they hurry toward the grain bins or vie over an especially attractive spot in the shade, and the disbudding process saves the herd from any danger an aggressive, horned doe might present. In a quick, simple process an iron, heated to cherry-red by a blow torch, is applied twice to the crown of the head, destroying the two roots from which the horns would grow. Before being released, an antiseptic, cooling salve is applied to the kid's burns, and soon after a scab forms and the hair grows in place.

Despite the rational explanations I heard and my general acceptance of all the practical aspects of farming, I never grew accustomed to the sudden bleat of the kid as the iron touched him, nor to the smell of burning flesh which spread throughout the basement where the infant kids were brought for a few days after birth and where the disbudding took place. Whenever I saw the tools being brought forth and the kids assembled, I would head for the mountainsides intent on hunting for lady's slippers and other wild flowers in the cool moist areas. Returning to the house hours later, flowers in hand, the scent from the disbudding would be lingering in the downstairs rooms, and the kids would look strangely like owls, at their play once more, their heads scarred by the two round burns larger than their eyes.

For several years we took the goats to shows in the summertime, settling them into the back of our station wagon with straw, hay and a supply of grain, as Buppong bid his farmers good-by for the day. The trips to the local shows were a great lark for John Carl and me, and we would look forward to packed lunches and all the excitement that goes with new grounds and people and the ribbons and small trophies of the ring.

Sometimes we went along, too, when the goats were taken to the railway station to be shipped to a new owner. They

Gramma accepting Brocade's third Grand Champion award

were sold to breeders throughout the nation and abroad, usually for sixty-five to one hundred and fifty dollars each, the price depending on the dam's production records. We would leave the kids in their crates, bedded deeply with straw, where the caretaker and an express attendant had lifted them onto the pushcarts next to the railway platform, gazing after the ones we had played with and knew so well. I learned early that it was the way of farming for animals to be bought and sold, live and die, to meet the farmer's need.

In the evening, after milking, we sometimes spoke of the goats we had bid good-by to that day and of their future homes. We would stroke the ones that were left behind with us, and we would often linger for as long as possible in the barnyard, waiting for dusk to fall, talking, sitting along the stone wall that formed an arc around the old elm tree there.

some proclamations to an old stump

me for Thoreau and the nine bean rows

me for the simple life

me for spring-kids nuzzling my fingers

me for the first radish-thumb to crunch

me for the wash-line at soft-smelling dawn-grey

me for the candle lit when the room reaches dark muddles

me for my hands in the damp black earth transplanting green-
      yellow lettuce leaves

me for a baby in the middle of the night tugging at
      one breast while milk flows from the other

me for the eyes of the grey work team

me for a man to bring delight—to warm crisp sheets
      on singing winter nights

me for the morning-glory on the garden fence in warm-dusk

me for the quiet mind to meet pain cool

me for a hollyhock at 5 a.m. in the sunrise

I sing the simple life

I sing the nine bean rows

—HELGA SANDBURG
Connemara, 1948

The country life...

Despite several articles carried by local newspapers which announced the family's move to Connemara, the Sandburg clan arrived at the new home with little notice from the townspeople and mountaineers. We were now living in a part of the country that placed farm know-how above literary merit. Our first bill came addressed to: "Mr. Sanborn, c/o Connie Mary, Flat Rock, N.C."

Here in these mountains the poet could find relief from his frequent lecturing tours. Some years after moving to Flat Rock he told his friend Ralph McGill, "A man must find time for himself. Time is what we spend our lives with. If we are not careful we find others spending it for us. . . . It is necessary now and then for a man to go away by himself and experience loneliness; to sit on a rock in the forest and to ask of himself, 'Who am I, and where have I been, and where am I going?' . . . If one is not careful, one allows diversions to take up one's time—the stuff of life." These hills were willing to give Buppong the time and the solitude of which he spoke.

But for the farming members of the family, the need was

instead to absorb all we could of the country life. The name "Connemara" was immediately expanded to "Connemara Farm," and the new stationery arrived with its letterhead, "Connemara Farm, Chikaming Herd of Officially Tested Dairy Goats, Flat Rock, N.C." On the stationery especially designed for the Toggenburg sector of the herd there was a small photo of four prize does' hind quarters—showing their productive udders.

John Carl and I soon were wearing T-shirts bearing the words "Chikaming Goat Herd, Connemara Farm" and the massive head of a buck goat in red in the center. Our first herdsman, Frank Mintz, Jr., had urged Helga to order these shirts in all sizes, using them as a uniform for his square-dance team at exhibitions at the Mountain Dance Folk Festival or at the Apple Festival at harvest-time. In between these appearances, our barn garage was often cleared and equipped with a stand, chairs, refreshments and crepe-paper decorations for Saturday night barn dances. The Sandburg adults rarely participated in these dances, but we children often were allowed to attend. I would watch anxiously while Helga and the men completed the milking and then cleaned the milking room and milk house, sweeping and washing the concrete floors and white doors neatly stenciled by Helga: "No Smoking," "Keep door shut," "No dogs allowed." Then I would go to the huge, empty garage to wait for the men and women who would begin arriving as dusk fell. The men came with watered-down hair, their weathered faces smiling as the greetings were exchanged, "Hey, hi you!" "Why, where you bin?" Their arms often went across each other's shoulders in a familiar gesture of friendship I was rarely to see after I left the mountains. The women would gather to ask each other about their "young uns" or whether the family was going on the church outing.

"Reckon we will, if we ain't plumb tuckered out," would come the reply.

Everyone brought their children. The boys and girls gathered in mischievous groups to plan what games they would play or to exchange secrets. John Carl and I joined these children with some envy over the knowledge that our friends rarely had to go to bed before their parents. We sensed their freedom, their tough independence that was hampered only rarely by a hickory stick or razor strop.

Soon the herdsman's rhythmic calls would fill the night along with the sound of the dancers' flying feet and the band of guitars, banjos and an accordion or harmonica. The garage was open-sided and across the driveway the cornfield and vegetable gardens spread out toward the mountains, Little and Big Glassy. We stayed up late at night and saw the night sky darken over the lighted, singing building and the fields and quiet hills. At last Helga would come, perhaps with one of my aunts or with Buppong, to walk with us up the road to our beds. If Buppong accompanied her, he might ask for a harmonica tune which the player would be proud to give. The mountain people liked the way my grandfather saluted them. "He ain't one bit uppity! He's a perty good feller, he is," they would declare. And Buppong would murmur as we headed back to the house, "Guess I better get my harmonica out again. That man knew how to coax out a tune!" And then Helga and he would talk in low tones of the slip of pale moon they sighted above the woodshed, or of the scent of narcissuses from the spring garden on our right. Helga might tell him of the sight she had seen that day, of which she had written hurriedly in her journal, "Incredible! A goldfinch in the pink dogwood!" John Carl and I walked between them stilled by the sudden quiet after the evening's play. We felt that somehow our family might be different from the mountain and farm people. There was a different accent noted even by us when Helga or Marne would gently advise, "It isn't 'Ah bin down yonder. . . .' Say, 'I've been in the lower pasture . . .' "; and we knew our family talked more about world affairs than the caretaker did; but we rarely compared the merits of one way of life with the other. Perhaps the only exception to this occurred on the morning that I tasted hot corn bread mixed with butter and molasses at the Mintz's home. Sitting at their table with the wood stove beside me and the sweet food before me, I felt no way of life could equal this one.

Like Helga, I was eager to participate in all aspects of farming. I watched the butcherings; the blood spurting forth still hot from the neck of the newly slaughtered creature, hung by its hind legs from the walnut trees in the lot which held the corncrib. I marvelled at the skinned creatures, never going close like my older brother, but awed at the rhythm and line of the muscles and sinews exposed to sight.

One warm morning, after the unforeseen death of a particularly valuable buck, an autopsy was performed in a small room of the buck quarters. The adults watched carefully as the vet cut open the bloated belly in an attempt to discover the cause of death. "Are you sure you want to stay?" they asked me. "She's a real little farmer!" The room was full of a sick and gaseous stench, the straw slowly becoming sodden with the belly's juices. I was one of the last to go, impressed with what I had seen, and even more impressed with what one had to go through in order to be called a "real farmer."

There were, however, other, more pleasant ways of commanding the respect of the men who worked the land and stalked on it in huge, greased leather boots. Early, it was discovered that I was afraid of no animal, and, as often follows,

Pearl and Major with the herdsman

few animals were afraid of me. When the first spring plowing was to be done, the farm hands and Helga took me to the low pastures where the huge, winter-loose Percherons were grazing, wary of the work that might lie before them if they allowed a halter to be slipped over their heads. What gentleness they showed me as I pulled the leather around their gigantic faces and held them still for the waiting men to lead away! It must have seemed amusing to the farmers for beasts weighing a ton apiece to obey a four-year-old child of some thirty or forty pounds, but for me it formed a basis for trust in creatures which I have never lost.

After the greys were harnessed and plowing the fields, I often took my toy animals out to the newly turned land and played where I could watch Pearl and Major move steadily on the soil, breaking up the roots and pulling stones to the top, forcing the land to accept the farmers' corn kernels and wheat and rye seeds and soy beans. The man who guided the plow behind these two, shortly before so reluctant to leave their leisurely life, had only to sling the reins about his bare shoulders now, and call out "Gee" or "Haw" to the Percherons

—or an occasional "Gee damn the shafts done busted!" which would put the horses back in a near pasture again, to crop grass under the afternoon sky, until man had repaired his invention.

Storm and Paula

Horses took on a special meaning for me at Connemara. I was the smallest person on the place and they willingly made it possible for me to be as tall or travel as fast as anyone else. I soon moved from my lead pony, Patches, who had been brought to Connemara in the back of the station wagon, to a tall chestnut-sorrel gelding named Storm. Storm had once been a five-gaited show horse, and there was a story which greatly appealed to me that told of his last ring appearance and the applause and tears of the crowd. He was about fifteen years old when Helga first purchased him for her own use. He was a favorite saddle horse of hers for two or three years. Then, trusting his intelligent ways, she gave him to her four-year-old daughter. He was my infinitely gentle companion for three years, until, at twenty, he began to limp badly, losing weight as he found it difficult to move around the pastures. Unwilling to see him so miserable, Helga skillfully shot him in the temple. He was buried in a far pasture beneath a group of pines, his death marking the first real drama in my short life. When Buppong asked me to write a story for him at that time, I printed clearly, "Once a upon time. when i was a little girl. Only 3 years old. they called me Snick. I learned to ride horsebak. My horse was Named. Storm. I loved Storm. But when I was 7 he dide."

When I first became Storm's owner, I was presented with a child's Western saddle which perched securely on his tall back. Helga put braids of brightly colored ribbons in my mount's bridle, as she did with all the horses, and she often placed flowers in his foreband before seeing us off. I sometimes took him to small local horse shows with an older neighbor, my clean blue jeans topped with a secondhand dress-jacket of John Carl's, my braids pulled tight at the base of my neck. We won a few handmade ribbons and some praise from people who smiled to see such a casually outfitted pair enter the ring with such confidence, but the greatest excitement was in the idea of a day's journey beyond Connemara's boundaries and the provisions it necessitated—the halter and lead slung around my waist, and the currycomb, brush and grain packed carefully along with my lunch.

Young, I fell often and easily when Storm tripped while cantering on Connemara's stony paths or when he shied at a rabbit in the field. I was never seriously hurt, however, and have never feared that dizzy knowledge that my balance is lost and I am falling. I was reckless with horses, and the lack of fear protected me, for I fell intent only on rolling to my feet and recapturing my horse. One time in particular I recall racing down the rocky road to the barn, when Storm reared to one side to avoid some barking dogs. I fell, hanging determinedly to one rein. Looking up, I saw that he was rearing—turning in order not to strike me with his hoofs. As always, the incident cemented an almost mystic faith in adventure, rather than discouraging it. It was not long before I urged Storm to rear on command, as Helga had taught him to do. The family would obligingly assemble at the dining room window to watch our act, and Storm would politely perform.

Together, Storm and I travelled over the mountain trails and grew familiar with country roads and driveways. We confronted snakes at times, and barking dogs and friendly people along the roadways. Once, riding with Helga on the Little River Road, we had to back out of the way to let a large truck pass by. Winding beside the road was a deep, narrow ditch, and, as Storm lost his footing backing off the road, I felt the two of us falling into this cleft. Helga lifted me off, but it was impossible for Storm to get out of the ditch, the muddy walls too sheer and slick for him to find footing. Cars stopped and people gathered along the road. I stayed at Storm's head, calming him, listening to the shouted advice of the passers-by: "Shoot him! You'll never get him out of there without a broken leg!" "How you gunna haul him out, lady? You can't get a plank down there."

But Helga found one man who would ask for help as he went through town, and in an hour's time a crane and sling were brought to the scene. Helga secured pieces of leather about the horse's belly and in time we watched Storm hoisted from the ditch, his hoofs striking the air in an attempt to find footing, and the onlookers exclaiming, "Well, I'll be dogged!"

When I was six and Storm began showing his age clearly, Helga decided it was time for me to have a young horse of my own to train in my own way. He arrived one day—young and splendid—with slender legs and alert ears which he flicked daintily as we rode, taking in all the sounds of the countryside. He had a flaxen mane so beautiful against his dark sorrel coat that I wished never to forget him. I named him Remember. Helga was busy with her own varied mounts, and so the care

of Remember, his feeding and grooming, was relegated to me. I stood on a box to carry out my chores—spending long hours combing out his shining mane.

Gramma or Helga often handed me a packed lunch which I would carry on horseback to some rock or glade on the mountain. I liked my solitude and the sound of the horse nibbling over leaves at a short distance, and the independence I had declared. This powerful new feeling evidently had its trying effects on the family when I returned home in the evenings. My grandfather typed in detail one evening:

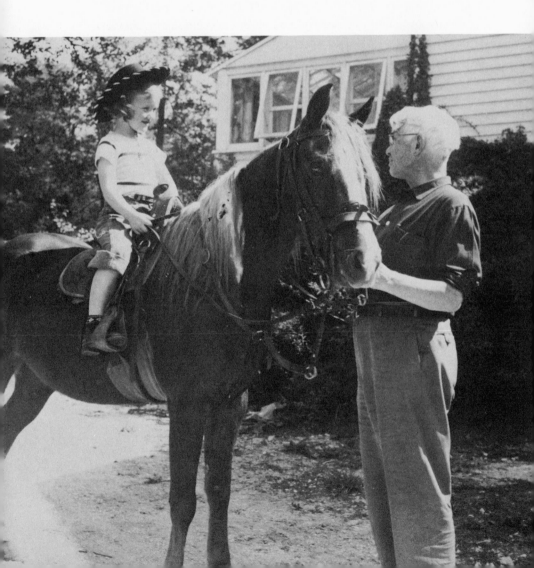

"Privately, and just between you and me and the pate-ghost, I believe Snick sometimes thinks she is a queen. The big lights were on in the Farm Office. Snick in a blue nightgown, wearing a white towel as a cape over her shoulders, suddenly spoke. With commanding vehemence and an authority she knew no one would dare dispute, her voice rang out: 'Don't waste electricity.' Then she marched five proud steps to the light switch, turned off the light, took three quick steps to the door, stood there with a bright smile of complete royal assurance, her chin drawn in, looking at her grandmother and grandfather seated at the table. She was unquestionably satisfied that she had done a good deed, that she had performed a service in behalf of household economy and efficiency. Snick has been learning how to issue commands. Large cumbersome horses, equine creatures fifty times her size and weight, powerful, four-legged beasts such as the dignified chestnut Storm—she commands them and they obey her. So she has been getting queenly and queenish when away from her horses. When she now cuts loose with the command, 'Don't waste electricity,' she means it and will require obedience or know why. From now on we may expect to see her act as the sworn foe of the Duke Power Company. Those who waste electricity will hear from Snick."

We kept the horses on pasture generally, but during the cold and storms of winter, we brought them into a part of the barn. There the creatures would find mangers of field hay and a portion of grain. The name of each horse was painted on his stall: Pearl, Major, Grey Boy, Blueberry, Kentucky, Paper Doll, Daniel, Storm, Remember. The caretaker's children, Betty and Frankie Mintz, had dogs and horses, too, so we often rode and explored together. And at times Helga accompanied me up the mountainside, perhaps riding her wild gelding, Kentucky, or the black mare, Bess, who had a massive,

59

Remember and Paula

trailing mane and tail and a colt, Nicker, who would lie down on the sunny slopes blowing softly when we paused to rest the horses.

Occasionally a caravan of riders—all the family except Gramma and Buppong—and friends would ride through the mountains in search of blackberry patches or blueberry stands. Once, with berry pails swinging wildly, the entire troop beat a hasty and painful retreat down the mountainside after the horses had walked into a low-hanging hornets' nest. The wild-eyed animals had to be soothed and reassured that the droning insects had been outrun. Set loose in the pasture, some of them turned to the muddy bank of the small lake there, to ease the swollen places. The humans then trooped into the kitchen to make saucersful of a cool, smooth paste of baking soda and water to apply to their reddening lumps of skin.

With the seasons' change the family's baskets filled with different harvests as we rode on the mountain paths. In November the three persimmon trees halfway up Big Glassy brought forth their tiny, bronze-colored fruit, each bare limb laden heavy. We learned to avoid eating the skins and to be certain that the fruit was fully ripe before we plopped it in our mouths. Sometimes, too greedy, John Carl and I would suddenly pucker up our faces, spitting the unripe fruit unceremoniously before us to search anxiously for a spring or pool of rain water where we could rinse away the thick, cottony feeling left on our tongues.

Before Christmas, we would walk the pastures recalling where we found the mistletoe the year before, and plucking the waxy galax leaves from the sides of the paths on Little Glassy. In town one could buy wreaths made of the leaves, which turned from dark green to deep maroon as the holidays approached, but we preferred to lay our own among the bright china-red bittersweet berries, and among the holly which we broke sparingly from the gigantic tree by our kitchen door. We left a profusion of that tree's fruit for the squirrels, and for the pileated woodpecker. Sometimes, just before our own meal, Helga would call us to see the bird, with his crest of red feathers and large speckled body, perching high among the prickly evergreen leaves bent heavy with snow, making his own holiday meal on the brilliant berries.

". . . if I live to be an old witch's age
yet will I return in time
to need the earth
part of a miracle. . . ."

—HELGA SANDBURG
Journal, 1947

Helga with her dog Jackson and Brenda

Helga...

"To a woman like me spring is an insatiable passion—a fierce tender terrific thing. . . . " Helga wrote these words in one of the journals she kept while living at the farm, perhaps at a time when she was setting thousands of strawberry plants into the April earth. She never seemed to tire of seeing what new things our land would accept; she kept Connemara in a constant state of change. Perhaps it is the winters that a farmer spends unable to tend to his soil that stores up in him the desire to plant the new crops. Over the winter months our house filled slowly with stacks of gardening catalogs and books containing crop advice from the Department of Agriculture. Helga would study these pages as intensely as John Carl and I absorbed the toy section of the Sears, Roebuck catalog, and, as the winter months disappeared, orders were decided on and filled. One day Gramma would bring from town seed packets, seedlings and mysterious dirty bulbs she had bought from the feed store or market, and at the barn I would discover the bags of lime, fertilizer, garden and field seeds which would mark the re-establishment of Helga's pact with the soil. The work horses, Pearl and Major, would be hitched and would pull the spreader behind them slowly, leaving a dust of minerals on the land that would prepare the field for its new crops.

The animals and the crops were rotated from field to field as the years passed. Running to the plot of land where last year the corn grew high and bronze-tasseled, I would surprise a herd of wary sheep. Startled, they would make short bleating noises and set the bells ringing on their wide collars. Pushing against each other's shoulders, they would halt at a safe distance and the leaders would turn with distrust in their eyes as the herd milled behind them. Twice that summer these new sheep would be sheared, the hired man pulling one from a pen and throwing it as Helga's deft hands guided the clippers deep into the matted wool. When the workers wiped their foreheads with damp sleeves and let the creature up at last, it would run back to the herd, slim and almost pink, the collar and bell seeming too heavy now. In time I watched the entire herd, shorn, grazing on the land again. I knew that they must be more comfortable now under the summer sun, but somehow I pitied them. They suddenly seemed so vulnerable in their nudity, their large dark eyes seeming oddly disproportionate. They reminded me more of water or night creatures—salamanders or flying squirrels, who would be defenseless deprived of the mud or dark—set beneath the sun in the middle of a field. I was glad to see their coats return in time.

Helga filled Connemara with animals. Soon the pastures were dotted not only with the grazing goats and flocks of sheep, but with the massive, quiet bodies of Black Angus as well. Near the back drive, where the crested wild iris and columbine bloomed profusely in spring, a pen of hogs was set up and slops and hog food were taken to it each afternoon, to the excited and then contented grunts from the beasts.

For some time the old laundry building was filled with hens, every year another breed to vary the pattern and to distinguish the age of the fowl—Rhode Island Reds, Plymouth Rocks, White Leghorns, Buff Orpingtons, White Rocks. John and I were often sent to collect the eggs from the rows of nest boxes which covered two of the walls of the small house. Egg gathering was very satisfactory, reminiscent of Easter when one found a score of eggs in one especially popular box. Some were still warm to the touch, and in the coolness of early morning I would clutch such a one in my hand as I continued the search.

Occasionally the decision would be made that it was time to slaughter the young cockerels or cull the hens, and a day would be set aside. Helga would be assisted in her task by Ella, our housemaid-cook, who had met the family shortly after they came to Flat Rock, and who was to work at Connemara for the next twenty-five years. She put pots of water on the basement stove as Helga arrived in front of the henhouse with a broomstick to dispatch the chickens in the way she had learned when she was young from her family's Indiana housekeeper, Martha. She held each chicken by the legs, laid the broomstick across its neck, pulled sharply—and the head lay on the ground. Then she threw the chicken a few feet off to flop headless for some moments.

When the headless bird lay still, Ella would plunge it into boiling water, pick the down and feathers, remove the crop and the viscera and the oil gland by the tail, peel off the gizzard lining—until there was a plump smooth body to be frozen for storage or eaten that night.

John Carl and I watched the slaughter eagerly the first time—anticipating the sight which Ella had depicted so clearly in the week just past—of a chicken running about headless. I don't know if I ever saw the actual sight, but I have a vivid picture of it in my mind. Ella had a way of describing things quite graphically. Sitting down to my mashed potatoes in the evening she would inform John Carl and me, "Now my daddy used to spit on the arsh'taters while he was chewin' tobacco, so as the young uns wouldn't take more'an their share."

Helga settled a flock of ducks in a pasture pond, too, and we gathered eggs from them sometimes and rarely they provided us with a meal. In the same pasture she put a part-Hereford calf one year, and appointed me its caretaker. My duty was to feed it each evening from a bucket fitted with a long black rubber nipple. As the calf grew, I began to regard it with a measure of animosity. It would wait at the gate as I neared, crowd me as I slipped into the pasture and then suck loudly as it drank, nudging the bucket with increasing violence as it grew. Several times it hit the bucket with such force that the milk splashed and soaked my entire six-year-old figure. Steadily dwarfed by the once-small calf, my only retaliation could be a furious, "Wait until I eat you," which in time I did with some relish.

Across the driveway from the barn lay the open fields where Helga and the caretaker's family grew their vegetable gardens. These two fields had been elaborate terraced gardens when the family first arrived at Connemara. Dying boxwoods had seemed to speak of days when slaves kept the turf smooth enough for ladies to stroll elegantly down the cultivated paths from the big house to this last bit of civilized grandeur lying level before the rise of the two mountains. All the boxwoods of these fields were gone now. The few living plants had been given to Christopher Memminger's relatives, and the rest had been burned or plowed under when we first arrived at Connemara.

Manure was brought from the barn and spread over this land and seeds were sown. Helga bent to the customs of the mountain folk—always listening if they advised planting or reaping in a certain phase of the moon. She noted in her journal, "All squash, cucumbers, watermelon, gherkins, pumpkins, melons planted day before May first. As Mintz figures, it can't hurt to put them out the day before. Just so they are in before sunrise May 1. Important!"

It was on the rise just above these vegetable gardens that the strawberries were set in one year. In rows stretching two hundred feet, the spaced small plants grew until they were a continuing mound of lush green leaves. John Carl and I were sometimes conscripted to weed the strawberry patch and finally to pick the ripe fruit. From May to midsummer, we filled our long baskets with the heavily scented berries. The hot sun burned our bare arms and legs as we moved down the rows on our knees. When the biting insects became too much of a trial we would turn for home, our legs and shoes bearing a coat of earth, and our lips stained as red as our fingers from the portion of hot, sweet berries that had never made our baskets.

The following year Helga gave up the strawberry patch as more trouble than it had been worth—and so the strawberries grew wild for a season. We children still went there—without baskets—to hunt for fruit or sit on the rise in the late sun and play with our legion of stuffed animals where the air was always scented with the berries. As with orchards in fall, the fragrance held us, and, as if we had been directed to stay among the strawberries, we lingered there until the fruit was gone. On the same rise, that second year, Helga set her beehives. We watched her, dressed in white with a wide protecting hat of net, go to the hives and lift out the supers of honey as the bees droned steadily about her. The honey was sourwood and clover. Helga and Ella would pack it respectfully in jars and coated cardboard containers. My grandfather put honey into every cup of his coffee and the family often ate it with butter melting on the first hot slices of Helga's bread loaves just taken from the oven.

Gramma's brother, our Uncle Ed, once said to the family, "Helga has all that Thoreau had except she doesn't have to live alone." Though she ran an efficient dairy, she seemed to prefer to raise plants, animals, children without excessive supervision. Her herb garden, set in a corner of the once-formal Spring Garden, grew wild and overgrown by August, not so much through neglect as through Helga's desire to have things in their natural state. It was a fine garden, wild as it was, and we watched or followed her often as she gathered her basil, coriander, borage, parsley, sage and thyme amongst the young honeysuckle vines and ragweed.

Helga had a life separate from the farm people too—she formed a Chikaming Siamese cattery at the house and raised Doberman pinschers; and she typed my grandfather's manuscripts and took down the letters he dictated in a special shorthand he had taught her, typing them up for his signature. She spent hours on the side porch painting portraits of her father in repose, or wild-eyed children, oils of Van Gogh suns over beaches, and pastels of apples, oranges and fields. She wrote poetry too, and kept a journal. And she bound books, and studied the stars, read widely and worked with sheet metal.

She let her two children grow without much supervision, leaving them free to explore the land, to invent games together and to discover new trees to climb. So it was that John Carl and I knew the land intimately, and that I grew to view it as a being, a companion—almost a parent. As dusk fell, Helga would call her rambling children in for the evening meal, often laughing as she heard them telling reckless tales of what the day had given to them. At last, she would put us to bed with a story of A. A. Milne's or E. B. White's, reading softly by a light just outside the bedroom door. I would fall asleep exhausted and always anxious for dawn and the scent the morning air would bring again—of the animals and the land.

The only serious spanking I ever saw John receive from our mother was when he spoke discourteously to his grandfather one evening. The air was thick as Helga led him from the table where he had been sitting. "If I *ever* hear you speak that way again . . ." And the most clearly remembered reprimand she gave to me was after I had neglected my duties as the guinea pigs' caretaker, and it sat heavy within my stomach. "They will die if you forget to water them—and *you* will be responsible."

Helga had dark hair, tanned skin, grey-blue eyes and, as was the case with her parents and sisters, broad, capable hands. She used to laugh, looking at them, "Well, we're all

Helga on Grey Boy

of peasant stock—and that's the healthiest, you know!" I have two sharp mental pictures of her in those farming days. One is of her active about the barn, surrounded by the creatures, always able, and doing more work than any of the hired men. The second image is of her at twenty-eight years of age, in a full-skirted silk dress—white with navy polka dots. It was at the railway station and she was on the baggage car between the open doors, just having returned from Florida with the new Doberman pinscher puppy, Lief. She seemed unbelievably pretty as she hopped down from the car, the puppy in her arms, her dark hair and skirt flying in the wind. The railway men whistled and called their appreciation, and I felt exuberant at the thought that she was related to me.

She had callers while we lived at Connemara, though John and I were never particularly aware of them. When she went out in the evenings, Helga would feed us supper early, at a blue, low table set in our bedroom's bay window with a red and white check tablecloth spread over it. Once, after I had gotten into bed, one of Helga's callers presented me with a stuffed Kanga and Roo, which I received with all the reserve and underlying excitement due two new friends. They were to be among my favorite toys in years to come, accompanying me on rides. Roo was lost in a cornfield one whole summer until a worker rescued him and set him high on a fence post for me to find.

In the last weeks of summer she would take John and me to the county fairs, where we looked at all the farm animals, flower arrangements, baked goods and preserved fruits and vegetables. The grounds were filled with the scent of cotton candy, taffy apples and popcorn, and I predictably fell in love with the merry-go-round while John bought tickets on all the more exciting rides. At last, tired and holding with

our sticky fingers some prize we had won, we came home from
the fair in the station wagon, dozing on the back seat, listening
to Helga singing to herself in front:

> *Somebody's tall and handsome,*
> *Somebody's brave and true,*
> *Somebody's hair is very fair,*
> *Somebody's eyes are blue!*

JOHN CARL

I have seen thee in solitude and
self-communion.
Thou hast wandered in thought
and reverie seeking great meanings.
I trust now this early the integrity
of thy mind and its searchings.
Freckles thou hast and a moonrise
smile and I value these phenomena
as precious possessions.

—CARL SANDBURG
Connemara, 1946

Dana Steichen

John Carl

My brother...

The summer gone, John Carl and I spent more and more time in the orchard. The apple trees were set in the V of the tip of that last piece of flat land that lay at the foot of the two Glassy mountains. From the rocky slopes came fresh spring water, flowing into a clear stream which continued to weave itself like a bright blue thread into the greens and golds of our field patterns and on to the two lakes. In the orchard, the stream was busy cutting into the granite of Big Glassy's sheerest slope. The mountain rose at a seventy-degree angle from the clear water, bare for quite some distance except for the shimmering spring water on the granite surface which gave the mountain the name of Glassy.

We children often played in the shade of the trees that grew alongside the stream. The orchard was kept smooth by a few docile cows held captive by the rise of the mountain and fencing on three sides. The caretaker's children and my brother were bold with adventure and often led the way over the stream and up the rocky slope to find nut trees, lizards or snakes. I followed my older companions with occasional cries of "Wait, wait, I can't go that fast!" My brother was my staunch supporter, always patient with his blond sister, so insistent on doing everything that he did. We had a strong bond in those earliest years.

My brother's nose and cheeks were thick with freckles in summertime, and he was solemn and droll—my leader. To Ella's amusement, he would sometimes bake cakes and make preserves as I sat watching him on a long-legged kitchen stool. Too young to master the problem of doubling recipes, John Carl always made two separate batches of batter or jam when he wanted a large amount. His cakes were delicious and only rarely lopsided, and Ella would beam at her curly-headed apprentice. "If he'd a'baked one fer the fair, he'd sure a'won the prize!"

At the top of Big Glassy, near the spot where Roger Hill's mausoleum had been standing since it was built soon after the turn of the century, perpetually maintained by a bank in Hendersonville, John Carl one year selected the best berries from a wild-blackberry patch, to make a pot of jam for Uncle Ed. He cleaned, sugared and cooked the berries with the same serious air with which he assembled erector sets and disassembled clocks. Standing on the small stool he used for cooking our breakfast eggs, he studied the boiling pot until its contents reached the precisely proper consistency, then poured it into the sterilized glass. After sealing it with paraffin, he stood triumphant with one pint jar of jam—the result of a long afternoon and a kitchen strewn with sugar, containers, sticky spoons and ladles, paraffin boxes and blackberry stems.

To insure that the jar would not break in the mail, Gramma wrapped it in her inimitable way—secure with ample string and shock-absorbent materials. Her wrapping was a source of admiration to the rest of the family. Margaret and Helga would watch her and smile at each other. "We'll never starve

—we can always wrap packages for a living!" And Uncle Ed was to tell the family on his next visit, "I thought someone was fooling me. There was box within box within box, and at last the pint jar of John Carl's jam—which was excellent!"

These days were just before the years when John Carl and I would grow quite different from each other: I, absorbed in nature's visible products—plants and animals—emotional, unquestioning, accepting what my senses brought to me; John Carl, intent upon the sciences, always questioning and scornful of his sister's dreamy faith in creatures. "Aw . . . wait until the tractor replaces the horse!" he would soon tell me with an air of superior knowledge. "Or the helicopter! Horses will be extinct!" John Carl never lost his inborn respect for machines, electricity, chemicals. He began to repair light fixtures and assemble phonographs, concoct explosives and learn the intricacies of the atom while I turned to reading and long explorations of the hills with my grandfather, or alone.

Before the age of separation, however, there were the days when John Carl took his bear, Pooh, to the upper of our bunk beds just as faithfully as I took my troops of animals: Monkey, Gorilla, Kanga and Roo, Dumbo and Pinky the Horse, into the lower bunk with me. During these years we spent long hours together in our cave formed by the fifteen-foot-high, domed boxwoods, or climbing into the uppermost limbs of the great *Magnolia grandiflora* at the side of the house. The magnolia was sturdy, its limbs closely placed. We reveled in the feeling of height we found in this lemon-scented, spreading tree with its broad, glossy leaves of dark green and huge ivory blossoms. We rarely rested in the tree, more filled with a desire to feel our own agility proven as we swung among the branches like young animals and defied danger.

We were full of a feeling of independence too, that day we overheard Helga saying that the children would be taken to the dentist in the afternoon. John Carl was nearly six years old—not yet in school, but beginning to feel his ability to handle his own affairs. He told me firmly, "We are going to live on the mountain now—and we won't ever have to go to the dentist!" With forethought he put fruit and bread in our pockets and we set out for the orchard. Crossing the stream, we left the amiable cows to their captivity and moved up the mountainside to make a new home. John Carl was resourceful and we soon gathered enough wood to fashion a lean-to in a grove of scrub pines at the top of the granite slope. We planned for our future as we ate our provisions and looked down upon the fields, the barn, the orchard and animals, small below us. He was thoughtful, his eyes shining beneath his thatch of red hair. There were bees' nests on the mountain, he explained, and nuts in the fall—and we could sneak down the rock to get vegetables from the garden and milk from the goats. In the afternoon we dammed up a spring so that we would not have to go down to the stream for water, and we crept along the mossy trails establishing lookout points from which we could watch the farm activities below. I don't remember seriously thinking that anyone would be worried that we were gone. There was only the glorious thought that we had escaped fate and that the grownups would repent having thought of taking us to the dentist. Perhaps we felt that Helga would accept our going as she did the wandering of the male dogs. "It's their nature," she had said to us, and though she worried when they did not return for days, and sometimes went looking for them in the plank-sided station wagon, she was philosophical. "They will take care of themselves and come home when they want to."

In the early evening we heard calls from the land below us. "Butch . . . Missy . . ." Helga was calling us by the nicknames she had given us. Other voices came too—and we saw the family and the workers making their way over the land in all directions, cupping their hands to their mouths as they called. While it was nice to see everyone thinking of us, it was horrifying, too, to see so many people gathered on our behalf. We descended the mountain somewhat ingloriously, robbed of our new-found independence. As we crossed the stream, the searchers collected to inspect, question and reprimand us as the cows looked on with mild interest at this unusual gathering in their orchard. I was surprised to find Helga in tears—it was not the way she received the vagabond dogs at all. She took us home, gave us dinner and read to us as we fell asleep in the bunk beds, the stuffed animals lying wide-eyed beneath the blankets on either side of us.

We kept an appointment with the dentist the next week.

POEM FOR KARLEN PAULA

sweet child
what I said was
sweet child
and now I say it again
sugar   molasses   honey
and once more
which will be enough
potatoes   carrots   onions
     and I love you for the way
     you can eat while you talk
     and talk while you eat and
     I like it when you spill on
     your chin and once in a big
     long while I like to hear
     you slurrpp   slurrpp   your
     soup
why do you sweep me
     with your eyes?
can you see how I am swept
     when you sweep me
     with your blue eyes
     ever so blue
     ever so deep blue?
have I even once asked you a question
     and you didn't have an answer?
     no— NO   NO.

each and every time you had an answer
          maybe not the right answer
          but a fresh quick fast one
          and this is proper   right
          when it happens
          between you and me
          for you and I have a book
          together we have a book
          it is our own personal book
          and it says on page one
          on page five and fifty-five
          I Buppong ask any question
          you Snick make any answer
          and if anybody says
          my question is wrong
                    or your answer is wrong
          we bring out the book
          your book my book
          our personal book together
          each by each us by us
          we can show where it says
          we do what we do
          when we do what we do
          and it is proper   it is right
          the law says we can
          if we love each other a bushel
          and it is a big enough bushel

                    —CARL SANDBURG
                    Connemara, 1947

Memories of my grandfather...

My earliest memories of my grandfather are of a time before I could walk well enough to want to climb Connemara's mountains and explore her crevices and streams. As the only man in a household of four women and two children, Buppong almost seemed a father to me for the eight years that I lived at Connemara—though he had a grandfather's tendency toward leniency. We spent much time together as I was growing up. Helga noted in her journal one evening the sight she had glimpsed returning from the barn on a fall day—her blond daughter's small figure trailing the tall, white-haired one: "She follows Buppong's enunciations and lengthy words with care and delight. 'The road—to hell—is paved—with good intentions—war is war—peace is peace—if all nations—would settle their differences—each must—sacrifice some principle—'" And John would say to his mother, shrugging, knowledgeable, "I know where Paus'l gets that. From her grandfather, not her other father."

Buppong generally came downstairs in the late afternoon. He tended to his voluminous mail then, and read newspapers while he ate a meal of salad, some piece of meat or chicken, a glass of goat's milk, rye bread with butter and coffee with honey and a little milk. In his workroom downstairs, the magazines, boxes of letters, books and supplies would be piled high on all tables as well as on the floor. I looked forward to the time in spring when such a room would have to be cleaned —the floor waxed and the rug taken away to be beaten and freshened. The resulting chaos of boxes and stacks of paper-matter formed a perfect fort for John Carl and me to play in— fashioning all manner of imaginary roadways and bridges and enemy castles.

I often played around Buppong while he had his lunch— though never if he had a secretary there to work with him. With few exceptions he was infinitely patient with children, even when they were particularly obnoxious. He seemed to relish the pranks and asides that we indulged in over the years, recording such infamous remarks as, "I feel like tearing things to pieces, even important papers!" He noted such phrases on his old typewriter, and labeled them as well: "Sweet Anecdotes of Snick"!

BUPPONG: "Do you love me a million bushels?"
SNICK (*six years old*): "I love a million bushels anybody don't hit me."
BUPPONG: "John, I think I'll cut your ears off."
SNICK (*whispers in Buppong's left ear*): "Don't do that, then when he is scolded real hard he can't hear it."

On another piece of paper, Buppong would quote my brother, " 'You're the goodest man there is, not in the United States but in this house. I'll tell you how good you are. There's only one man gooder than you are and that's the President.' And still later, 'Is the President a good man?' "

Paula and Buppong in the downstairs workroom

I grew to like the smell of cigar smoke throughout the rooms where Buppong worked. From under the table I could watch my grandfather's feet, toes resting inward as he typed or read, and hear the sound of his work—the rustling of papers, the swift, penciled shorthand, the click of the typewriter. Around the room were thick lead pencils in cigar boxes and in orange juice cans which John Carl and I had covered with Christmas wrapping paper and presented to our grandfather at yuletides. There were also stacks of paper of every weight and grade—although the cheaper newsprint was by far the most popular with Buppong and his grandchildren. As I played with my stuffed animals or painted under the table, I felt that every house in the world was filled with typewriters and books and orange crates full of letters, and inhabited by a man whose toes turned inward, clad in their ancient shoes.

When the day was mild enough, Buppong often took his mail and reading to the porch, or the lawn, or to the great granite rock on the rise by the back of the house. These times were less hushed than the ones in the house—and he was more easily distracted.

I planted a moss garden by his work area on the rock, and I often appeared by his side, asking him to come and see a sight in the garden—brilliant crimson spores or a yellow toadstool that seemingly came from nowhere among the greens and quiet greys of the moss. He was appreciative— "It's quite a sight, Snick!"—and often before returning to his papers he stood on the rock, feet placed apart, and raised the huge oaken armchair over his head and into the air. He seemed of gigantic proportions at such times, although he was only about six feet tall.

Sometimes as I knelt by my garden repairing some damage an irreverent dog or wild creature had wreaked, I would hear a mockingbird singing close by the rock. His song varied every few seconds, liquid, incredible—it held me motionless. When the song was at an end, Buppong would solemnly reply to it, whistling his interpretation. I was envious of the way he could warble a note and vary his tune as the grey bird with its long white-tipped tail had done.

In the evening, as my grandfather returned to the house, he might find John Carl and me at the pool on the front lawn, sailing wooden ducks or boats—our clothing well soaked. If we asked him to perform, he would obligingly produce a knife from his pocket and flip it through the air from the back of his hand, having it land standing four out of five times, after a single, double or even triple flip. John Carl and I stood most impressed at the sight of a second skill—where Buppong sent the knife swiftly into the ground between his outspread fingers, faster at each round. He had a collection of knives all through the years, friends often sending him a new, unusual one; and he could perform the tricks with them until he was almost eighty-five years old.

Soon we would have to turn to the house for dinner. Leaving the lawn we would follow Buppong up Connemara's broad steps, often imitating the way he climbed any stairway in his later years, tapping the toe of his shoe lightly on each step just after putting his other foot down. It gave cadence to the climb, and a few extra moments to view the settling dusk, and it put off for a short time our appearance at the dinner table. For this I was glad. Along with naptime, dinner was a time I viewed with apprehension.

Unless there were guests, I generally sat down at the table on my grandfather's left and warily watched the papers or books he brought to the dining room and placed beside him. His custom was to read aloud after the evening meal began. The range of material that might hold me speechless in my chair was sweeping—and there was a corresponding range in my reactions—from a restless, defiant concentration on mischief or the destruction of my peas, to an intense delight in the words or songs being produced. It was at the dinner table, too, that I can recall receiving most vivid, conclusive reprimands from Helga. One evening with a clean linen tablecloth covering the extra leaves in the table, and wine glasses and many guests—I remember Helga's gentle gesture beckoning me to her side, and her whisper in my ear, "If you don't settle down immediately, young lady, you are going to be spanked in front of everybody!" Then she smiled and I returned to my seat—everyone wondering over my changed behavior. "What do you whisper in her ear, Helga?"

The family often sang in the evenings, John Carl or I running to fetch my grandfather's favorite guitar. He played songs that everyone knew, and a few that were too fast and

crazy for my lips to master. I would listen, doubtful, as the adults sang rapidly:

> *I had a horse and his name was Bill.*
> *And when he ran he couldn't stand still.*
> *He ran away one day—*
> *And also I ran with him.*
>
> *He ran so fast he could not stop.*
> *He ran into a barber shop,*
> *And fell exhaustionized—with his eyeteeth*
> *In the barber's left shoulder.*
>
> *Oh! what could you do in a case like that?*
> *Oh! what could you do but stamp on your hat,*
> *And your toothbrush—*
> *And everything that's helpless?*

There were two songs that Buppong and I often sang together not only after dinner, but on the mountain paths, harmonizing in different ways, playing with the notes and words. One was "The Riddle Song," and the other an old Gaelic ballad, "The Trail of the Yellow Fawn." Connemara was a Celtic name, and while there was no connection between her name and the tune, the two seemed inseparable to me. The creatures in the song seemed familiar to Connemara's springs and hillside slicks of rhododendron and mountain laurel, and often in a late summer dawn I witnessed the morning mist mentioned in the song. I sang in a child's voice while Buppong ranged high and low making the song something worth hearing and fun to sing:

> *I left my darling lying there, lying there, lying there,*
> *I left my darling lying there*
> *While I went to gather blaeberries.*

91

Snick
Dana Steichen

I followed the trail of the yellow fawn, yellow fawn,
yellow fawn,
I followed the trail of the yellow fawn
But I would not find my baby-o!
I followed the wee brown otter's tracks . . .
I followed the trail of the mountain mist . . .
But I could not find my baby-o!

Sometimes our guests would be songsters. I remember Jean Ritchie coming through with a slender greyhound, Lady Gray, that seemed a wonder to me alongside my amiable black cocker, Hannah. Frank Warner came with his strong echoing voice, and the family's friends, Bill and Marge Braye, came occasionally with Marge's guitar—and the evenings were full of song and the sound of guitars.

Music formed a large part of Connemara's life. When the guitar was still, the phonograph was often playing some piece of classical music. Buppong kept scraps of paper in a drawer upstairs on which he had noted in his shorthand the titles of works he had heard at a friend's house or over the radio. Beside them he indicated whether he should or should not buy a recording of the piece: "Concerto No. 1 Beethoven plyd by Gieseking: *Yes;* Saint-Saëns 4*th* pian cncrto C Minor—Robt Cadeseus at piano—Yes; Opus 42 Schubert piano = Schnabel, yes; Valse—Chopin = orchestra Kostelanetz = A-1; Capriccio Italienne Tchaikovsky—Yes; Rapsodie Espagnole: Ravel good Phila orch Ormandy; Symphony by Ralindikoff (Xtrdnry); Phila Orch EOrmandy Finlandia suprb; Czk Philharmonic Orch w Casals Cncrto fr cell B Minor Dvořák get!!!; Barber The Excursion Rudolf Serkin piano First of All!; duo fr violn & pian Roger Sessions No."

The folks at Connemara listened regularly, too, to the news. I recall the silence that Helga insisted John Carl and I keep during the half hour when the voice of Edward R.

Murrow was brought to the family by the booming of "A-M-A-C-O! Amaco!" The adults were concerned with politics and the state of the world. I didn't appreciate this concern, although I knew that Roosevelt was a name you handled with care and respect, that there were a lot of "damn fools" in the political world, that a few men were probably as fine and as good as some of our friends, and that in general it was a topic not to make jokes about unless you were pretty sure where everyone stood.

Buppong

John Vachon from *Look* Magazine, copyright © 1956, Cowles Communications, Inc.

John and I were led off to bed as a rule by our mother when "the political hour" came. Our last view of the family room would be of Buppong lying in the brown leather reclining chair, with its worn, broad oaken arms, his eyes shut in the dim light, listening to Murrow's resonant voice and the more distant, static-filled voices of the reporters around the world. At the dining table would be my Aunt Margaret and Gramma, with a look of concentration in their faces and postures.

None of the adults expected John Carl or me to comprehend what was heard on the broadcasts. In 1944 my grandfather wrote a piece called "Ever Normal Turmoil" which was concerned with political upheavals throughout the world and the necessary reactions to these occurrences that must take place within a free country. A few years later he inscribed one of these pieces for me with words that reflected Connemara's proportionate demands on the family members: "Dear Karlen Paula—my very own Snick—You were only a year old when the above was written. You were born in storm. And the storm goes on. . . . Will you please go on being a star and a flower? This is the hope and prayer of old cantankerous tantalizing teasing Buppong."

My perception of what interested my grandfather was on a more tangible scale than world politics. He enjoyed the drawings John Carl and I made, and the singing of songs, and the hours spent on Connemara's glassy sheets of granite rock. At a time when he might have been writing of the sweeping movements of armies and their generals, he also wrote for his three-year-old granddaughter: "When Snick runs she picks up one foot and puts it down in front of the other. Her feet keep time with each other. Each foot knows what the other is doing. She is proud of her feet. First thing she wakes up in the morning she asks herself, 'Where are my feet?' and puts her hands down to make sure her feet are there. Then she says quietly and decisively, 'My feet are good for me. Why, I wouldn't be without my feet for anything. When I get out of bed in the morning what do I do? I put my feet on the floor. What is the last thing I do before I get into bed at night? I take my feet off the floor. And I'll tell you a secret. Every night and every morning I thank God for my feet!' "

When I grew past the toddler age, I was occasionally allowed to go up to my grandfather's room around noontime to visit with him while he awoke, finished the food on the tray that Janet had set outside his door, and prepared for the day ahead.

All the rooms that he worked in were alike in the mounds of books, magazines and papers which filled them. Buppong did a great deal of reading, and I usually found him with a book, eating his breakfast in bed, surrounded by reading matter. I never saw him spill anything. I was amazed by the way he juggled the coffee and the milk and the books.

We often shared the fruit on his tray, and I would watch him eating oranges, peelings and all, without knowing where the habit had begun—proud of the way he ate oranges differently from anyone else I knew. Years later I was to read in *Always the Young Strangers* of his Christmases in childhood—the hard-working Swedish parents often giving only a five-cent bag of candy and a five-cent orange to each of their children. Buppong recalled in his book, "We honored the orange by eating all the insides, pulp and peelings."

I was drawn to his loftlike rooms. From the walks past Connemara's trees he had collected acorns, buckeyes, pine cones and hickory nuts which stood about the rooms in cigar boxes or crockery. He had a part of his collection of canes standing in a corner in a cardboard carton. Among them were dandies' sticks, hickory staffs and dark-stained canes with ivory handles. From the windows you could look over the tops of the boxwoods and the holly tree, the bamboo grove and the magnolia. You could see beyond the broad, flowering Obelia in front of the porch to the front lawn, the horses in the lake pasture and the road and mountains beyond. One wall of the bedroom slanted in like an attic, and that added to my feeling of being in a nest high above the earth.

The better part of one of the bedroom walls was covered with a billboard, which in turn was entirely covered with pictures clipped from magazines—some three layers deep. I would stand in front of that billboard an hour or more, studying the faces of Indians, the body of a dancer, processions of giraffes across an African countryside or ponies in the ocean off the shores of Chincoteague Island. Here and there on the billboard were magazine reproductions of paintings by Cassat, Picasso, Monet, Rembrandt, and a reproduction of Uncle Ed's photograph of his Brancusi sculpture, and the one of Rodin, Balzac, and The Thinker.

Buppong found pleasure in pictures of a fledgling crow crying for food, or a portrayal of a Chinese family gathered beneath a tree. We sometimes speculated about the people and countries and animals pictured on the billboard, and he would go to a drawer filled with pages ripped from magazines and put up a new scene—securing it with three or four thumbtacks.

Soon after he got out of bed he would turn on the record player, and as Segovia played Rondo and Theme by Sor, Buppong would tell me to take a book in each hand and lift them high as he did, lowering them to his toes, and then to each side. Every morning he did exercises before dressing and coming downstairs. Captain of his basketball team when he was in college, he stayed in good physical condition and delighted in the power and grace he saw in animals and in the farm people.

Buppong typing in his upstairs workroom

His workroom adjoined the bedroom, its walls almost obscured by ancient, heavy filing cabinets and bookcases. The pictures in this room were taped on the limited wall space, or thumbtacked to a board or piece of cardboard and placed on a shelf or cabinet. Buppong would carry with him on his travels an old brown envelope full of photos of the family and Connemara. He read or wrote while travelling by train and ate a lunch packed by Gramma or Helga: a bottle of goat milk, which he relished even when it soured, and a sandwich of thin dark bread heavily spread with butter and a thick piece of cheese between. In this way he avoided the waste of time a trip to the dining car would have meant. He preferred the simpler ways of life.

As a child of Swedish immigrants, Buppong's diapers had been made of flour sacks and the mattress he had slept on was a cornhusk one. Gramma, too, was born of immigrants, from Luxemburg. Their beliefs and their way of life were rooted in a faith and concern for the people and a love of the beautiful and simple things which they felt should be within the reach of every human being. In my first ten years I never examined the tolerance and concern which my grandparents showed toward the world. I only sensed that they were optimists, though realists, and I knew that they regarded nature in her continual change as somehow speaking of the potential in all forms of life.

Buppong's confidence in change was reflected in a phrase he repeated to me throughout a span of some twenty years. Putting together his letters and inscriptions, the phrase seems to have been a motif for our relationship. The first time he used it I was three years old, and it formed the entire message: "Snick me pixie pal," he began, "I love you not for what you are, nor for what you have been, nor for what you are going to be, but for all three. Buppong."

ADVICE TO A RARE SWEET CHILD

Let many lights spring forth on the sea for her.
Let the landpaths have many living crosslights.
Let her linger in seafog and read horizons.

The mystery of the sea
has a sister in her.
>   *The study of love requires seatalk.*
>   *How deep lies the seabottom?*
>   *Who told the seabirds how to travel?*
>   *What are the measures of bitter waters?*
>   *Does the sea be clumsy and gamble*
>   *for gain or the passion of chance?*

Always is a music to be sought out.
In the wood of a chair, a clothespin, an axhandle, a violin.
In the clink of ice on porcelain
Or the ring of a goldpiece on brass
In the travel and twist of lights in a globe of glass
>   *long moments all glass.*

—CARL SANDBURG
Connemara, 1950

Our million acres of sky

There is a stream of these darker moments...

My grandmother often exclaimed after mounting the twenty steps to the front porch and turning to look past the tall white pillars, "We didn't just buy two hundred and forty-five acres when we bought Connemara, we bought a million acres of sky, too!" At the front of the house the land sloped downward, and the horizon seemed low, distant, the sky immense. I would watch my grandmother's gesture toward the great expanse of blue, and would feel that perhaps the sun rose earlier and set later here than it did anywhere else—it had so much farther to go.

The rise and fall of the land in this hill country filled a day's wanderings with a rhythmic quality. Walking through the ravine of the buck pasture, one was surrounded by the land as if in a cavern, only a bit of sky fitting beyond the tree tops. Then, mounting the abrupt, steep hill beyond the buck house, coming to an enormous oak tree, the sky would be suddenly restored to its fullness. I could often look back from the vantage point by the oak to see a dozen bluebirds moving swiftly between the trees in the hollow I had just left, their small bodies bright in the sun, always seeming too beautiful somehow, as if they might have escaped from the lupine spikes in my grandmother's summer garden.

That ravine in the buck pasture holds another memory besides the sight of the bluebirds. One late summer a young Great Dane was brought home from the local veterinarian, who had seen in Helga the "good home" to which he had been authorized to give the dog. The Dane's new mistress named him Christopher and we became fond of him and of his clownish way of climbing onto the leather sofa and stretching his lanky body its full measure. He was gentle, playful, and our Doberman pinscher, Lief, accepted him with grace. The two were constantly at Helga's side, accompanying her to town and to the barn and the surrounding pastures as she rode, or milked and fed the herd. It was incredible to see one day in the autumn-blown buck pasture a pattern of bodies strewn before her, necks broken and bleeding—and Christopher still pursuing the few survivors. One of the highly prized buck kids lay with his skin unbroken in the tall warm grass, his eyes glassy and submissive with shock, never recovering.

John Carl and I watched from the gate as Christopher was beaten by Helga and hauled away to be locked up. The sight of him was no longer bearable to her and the next day he was returned to the vet. Lief, who had watched the killings with a puppy's fascination, was punished, too, as if he had done the deed himself, so afraid was Helga that he might be tempted to emulate what he had seen.

My brother and I spent a great deal of time out of doors on the rolling land. As with the rest of the family, we were used to the fact that quiet had to be maintained in the house during certain hours. Just as the vacuuming was always done in the late afternoon when the writer was outside, we children accepted the fact that no running or yelling was allowed past the glass doors that led to the hallway and the staircase over which Buppong's rooms could be seen. I only recall once or twice when my grandfather appeared, gripped the railing on the third floor and roared out, "Can't a man have a little quiet in his house any more?" We children usually had sped out the door as soon as our postlunch naps were over.

At the back of the house, among the runs that Helga had built for her Siamese cattery, John Carl and I had respective hutches of rabbits and guinea pigs. Every morning we watered and grained them, and I often took my favorite Abyssinian guinea pig to the little gazebo beside the fenced-in garden, which we referred to as the "summerhouse." Occasionally, our mother would call us away from our outdoor play, asking us to model for her on the screened-porch studio that adjoined her bedroom. Hoisting myself onto the tall chair, I would sit restlessly for what seemed an interminable length of time, interrupted regularly with the pleas, "Can I see now?" "How much longer?" "Haven't you got the nose yet?" Helga was patient, now and then coming over to place us back in the necessary position. Her paintings were rich with colors and her bold strokes went on with heavy brushes held fanlike in the same hand that gripped the palette. I liked her portraits of John Carl and myself. Though they sometimes seemed alien, I was drawn to the untamed look in the children's eyes. Their dark centers seemed focused on some distant thing known only to them, and the heads were often painted fullface, the chin uplifted, the gaze direct, as if the child was proud of his secret knowledge.

John Carl and I felt we knew the world whispered of in those portraits. We had experienced the strange excitement of roaming alone in the bamboo forest by the magnolia tree, treading in silence the slender fallen leaves which could be found nowhere else at Connemara. We had encountered a coiled rattlesnake among the lettuce leaves in the garden and then watched its death by the hand of the caretaker and the skin being nailed to a barn door. We had climbed the narrow winding stairs of the Swedish House and explored the piles of ancient dust-laden magazines and books stored there, dwelling on the musty scent of desertion. And I knew the sharp terror of pain. As a three year old, I had wheeled my tricycle into the lime-spreader one day and the long blade of the machine almost amputated my thumb—the proof still there in an irregular ribbon of pale skin nearly two inches long. My serious brother had wrapped the scarlet hand in his T-shirt, leading me along the drive from the barn to the house, assuring me that this was nothing to be kept as a secret in my fear of medical attention. I let him guide me to Helga's reassuring presence, but far back in my mind I stored the knowledge that in my hand was the same complex of muscle, white fat and blood that I had seen in the butchered animals hanging beneath the walnut trees.

Along with a wonder over the intricacies of my body, I had discovered the fact of mortality. On an autumn day when my Aunt Janet came racing to the house announcing her discovery, "Kitty Whispers has fallen into the icehouse!" I realized it was a question of whether the cat would live or die. The icehouse, another of Connemara's remnants from the Civil War era, was a twenty-foot, rock-lined pit covered with an angular slate roof, and designed to hold ice, cut from the lakes in winter, throughout the warmer months. The Sandburg family never made use of the icehouse in any way, and I had heard the caretaker speak of snakes living in its abandoned

John and Paula explore the cheese house

depths. I joined the spectators who watched Frank Mintz set a ladder in the pit and, armed with a flashlight, descend to rescue Janet's cat. Afraid to go near the rocky edge, I understood the courage the man had shown when he reappeared with the relieved Kitty Whispers.

Along with the shining memories of childhood, there is a stream of these darker moments, which often acquired significance in the powerful imagination of youth. Things that might seem to go unnoticed by a child are often stashed deep and silent in the workings of his mind. On a day nearly a year after World War II was over, John Carl and I walked toward the house down the long, bare rock, our arms filled with the stuffed animals we regarded so highly at that time. Reaching the mid-point of the rock, we stopped abruptly, sighting twenty-foot flames moving furiously up the hill from the lake. The hillside seemed alive with fire. I felt a helpless horror come over me as I watched the trees stand unmoving while the flames licked their trunks and branches with a yellow-white blaze of heat. We children fled, hugging the animals to us. Appearing before the family, five-year-old John Carl gasped out our conclusion: "The Germans are here! They've set fire to the hillside. They'll be at the house in no time."

The fire was at last defeated, not with guns, but with water, extinguishers and shovels. For a season the hill remained charred and the black tree trunks stood in sharp contrast to the falling snow of the winter months. In spring the family would recall the fire as we sat on the front porch, the new, light greens coming to the lake pasture and slowly covering the scars of the burned hillside. No one laughed at the children's interpretation of the fire, and, indeed, the adults soon forgot the incident. Yet, in years to follow, the fear of fire

107

The bamboo forest

advancing on timberland would come again and again to my dreams, as would other of the darker moments—the sight of a Dane coursing glassy-eyed creatures through a field, the unfamiliar depths of the ice pit. These had become as much a part of my memory as the rise and fall of the land and the sweeping sky.

"Yes, so simple we are, so little we want, we are wise and will get what we want."

—TO GRAMMA FROM BUPPONG
from a 1908 letter

"Three Acres and Liberty"...

When my grandparents were first married, they planned to live in a shack in the woods—with a roof, four walls, three chairs (one for company), a hat rack, a breadbox, a bowl for wild flowers and a coffeepot. They would call their place "Three Acres and Liberty." There was something of this same notion at Connemara, even though there were two hundred and forty-five acres and my grandfather was quoted as saying, "What a hell of a baronial estate for an old Socialist!"

The furniture the family brought along to Connemara was of mixed ancestry, and there were few pieces that anyone could have called important except for the service they provided. My grandfather often used orange crates instead of desks or tables. His workroom had one desk, a lamp, a chair, file cabinets and at least fourteen orange crates in it. They were versatile. He piled them one on top of another into bookcases, or he broke them down and spread them about, so he could see his work before him. On end they were the perfect height for two fingers to pick at the straddled typewriter in newspaperman fashion; and with their bottoms down they held endless stacks of manuscript in proper confines.

Throughout the rooms downstairs were sturdy tables where goat pedigrees, soil charts and stock inquiries could be spread out; and Buppong could read his daily mail, brought to the house from the post office each morning in large wicker baskets. Nowhere were there curtains or blinds. My grandfather slept in the morning with a scarf tied over his eyes; there was never more need than that to cut out the sunlight, and there was no one that we needed to stop from peering inside.

The farm was practical, a success, during those years when Helga managed it. It gave the family fresh milk year round, with the extra dividend of kids throughout the spring and summer to entertain us, dancing on their hind legs and leaping into the air at the slightest encouragement from the family. In autumn and throughout the summer the family would can and freeze vegetables and fruits for the winter months, and we made preserves and jellies from the wild mountain blackberries and blueberries.

The horses that carried us up the mountainsides on our berry-picking excursions were no extra expense, being fed on the grain and hay left over by the huge goat herd. In like manner, the dogs and cats were given milk, the leavings of the cheeses Helga made, and the bones and scraps saved for them when the cattle, sheep, or misfit goats were butchered.

Everyone at Connemara ate fresh, simple foods: thick soups and baked breads, fresh butter and cheese from our dairy. My grandfather seemed always as pleased by the color and aroma of the food set before him as he was by the taste of it. He was full of praise as Gramma brought his dinner, "No one can make a soup as good as you do, Buddy!" Lunch and dinner were times for Buppong to enjoy the family and share in the stories about the day's work. He never seemed to over-eat—usually ate slowly—and often he would miss a meal, saving a slice of pumpernickel bread for the afternoon, as he read or finished some piece of work he did not want to leave.

There were specialties at Connemara—Christmas cookies which Marne took charge of—filling the house with the scent of spices as sheet after sheet of pfeffernuss, anise, springerle and butter cookies came out of the oven. Gramma would bake fruitcakes in early December, Ella slicing the citron and candied fruits as John Carl and I watched my grandmother mixing heaps of currants and white raisins and nuts into the huge stoneware bowl already filled with butter, sugar, flour, molasses and spices. Ella talked continually the while, telling us of past Christmases and the customs the inhabitants of surrounding estates used to adhere to in the early part of the century. She called us "Little Carl" and "Pauley," and let us lick the bowls one by one as their contents emptied into the pans and onto the cookie sheets. Occasionally she would bake a pie for the family, but always declared that "Helger is the only one what can bake a cake!" More often than cakes, however, Helga produced fresh loaves of bread, which we children waited for eagerly—the butter and honey or jam already on the table.

There were rarely any sweets brought from town. The only candy we had, as a rule, was that sent to us by Mr. Hershey himself in large square boxes. My grandfather occasionally purchased some of his favorite sourballs, licorice or Chiclets, and they were stored with the Hershey bars in a cupboard in one of the front rooms, and in Buppong's working desk upstairs. Once in a great while, John Carl and I would plan a raid on the closet, my mind intent on the sweets. I was a bad accomplice however, since I ate the chocolate by melting it between my palms and licking the dark stuff slowly from my hands. It lasted longer that way, but the stolen goods hardly remained a secret.

Infrequently Helga took John and me into the department store or dime store in town and let us select one special toy. We could look forward to such an occasion whenever we were taken to visit our gentle family doctor, Dr. King, or if we had an appointment with the dentist. I never remember Buppong returning from a trip with a conventional present for his grandchildren, but he often brought mysterious gifts such as a Pullman Company pamphlet entitled, "Your Roomette and How It Works." He frequently sent me magazine clippings he thought I might like, of some grand horse and rider, or a wild animal caught in motion by the camera. If he was away on a trip and heard of a minor catastrophe, such a picture would come accompanied by a note: "Dear Snick— Your foot—Buppong prays for your precious foot. Buppong."

Buppong

He never dropped the custom of sending me magazine prints of photographs. Over the years, after I left Connemara, a collection grew and it fitted many moods. There were paintings of somber Hambletonian horses, noble emperors and covers from *Sports Illustrated,* one of a flashing horse in high regalia at Madison Square Garden, the words inscribed across it: "Snick—Where you and the horse get the gay glad rags you're wearing? We give you the highest award—Buppong."

In 1954, after my mother remarried and the new family had moved to Virginia, I received one day a picture of George Washington and his horse with the message, "Sweet Snick— It is dis Buppong who he say you shouldest be dis picture to haven & holden: man on horse guess what city dey name after him: how you ben dese days? dese daze? Bppng."

The next missive from him was a complaint which came in response to no response, and it contained Buppong's familiar phrase:

Dear Missy

You get by me in the United States mail General George Washington on a horse. From you I hear nothing about whether the general or the horse reach you. If only the general reach you I would like to hear about it. If the horse come and not the general, that I would like to know. And if both of them get lost so you have them not, maybe you will let me know. Maybe you do not get by me in the United States mail any General George Washington on a horse at all no time. Anyhow you are in my book and my humble estimation the prettiest and wittiest girl in the Commonwealth of Virginia, the Old Dominion, the Mother of Presidents. You should know that I am not in the habit of slinging around idle compliments and when I say I love you not for what you are nor for what you have been nor for what you are going to be but for ALL THREE, it is for you to consider and remember so sweeping a statement. I pray that your health is good. I trust that you make progress in your studies and that you have the same free and independent mind and will that I have always valued in you. I wish for many luck stars to be over you, says Buppong.

Another time he sent a newspaper photo of "A day at the races: Queen Elizabeth and her husband, the Duke of Edinburgh, resplendently attired for occasion, as they rode in an open carriage in procession around track at opening of Ascot race meet on Thursday." The Duke was wearing a high top hat and Buppong's letter read, "Dear Snick—If the Queen's husband offers to send me the hat he is wearing should I accept it and wear it to Washington and Falls Church? Would John wear it if I gave it to him? Ever sincerely Buppong."

At the University of Chicago, years later, during a time of examinations, there came through the mail to me a tiny battered volume of Shakespeare's *Twelfth Night,* which bore on its inside cover a large crayoned "10" attesting to the fact that it cost its buyer ten cents. On an inside page was written: "For Snick this rare and expensive book—with all the good wishes in the whole wide world Buppong."

My grandfather always had this knack of transforming the ordinary into the delightful. As we sat on the porch listening to dusk come to Connemara one night, he named the frog in the front pool "Archimedes." The creature always had a personality after that and his near primeval utterings no longer seemed strange to me. We saluted the frog, "And a good evening to you, Archimedes!"

On the front porch, too, one spring afternoon, my grandfather set a branch with three legs. On it he perched one of his floppiest hats and dubbed the new acquaintance, with its air of distinction, "Mr. McGuillicudy." When the branch was carried off by a dog weeks later, he threw a sweater over the back of one of the oaken armchairs, placed two bean boots at its base,

Mr. McGuillicudy

the hat on its back, and declared to John Carl and myself, "Mr. McGuillicudy is enjoying the view now."

A less friendly figure than Mr. McGuillicudy could be seen at the top of Little Glassy. There a limb with a great snout and open mouth and eye had been named the "Dragon Limb" by Helga and Buppong. We children looked on it with some awe and trod the dragon's domain with respect.

Many of the trees and flowers on the farm took on personality in a similar way. Looking at the pines under which the bird feeders stood, Buppong would exclaim, "How quiet they are today. Look at the hush! Not a movement out there. Not a leaf stirring." On a windy day, he would point out to the family or friends who were about, "Today the pines are speaking. Hello! How-do-you-do, gentlemen?" and he would add to one of us children, "They are our friends, I think!"

The Dragon Limb

In 1953, he wrote a poem called "Zinnia Sonata" and said it was "Written expressly out of sentiment and affection for Karlen Paula and John Carl, and the effulgent thoughtful zinnias who bloomed for the aforementioned persons in the summer of 1953 at Connemara." My grandmother had planted the zinnias in front of the house and they grew in a brilliant row which stretched the length of the lawn:

I have seen zinnias give out
with little songs and begging pardon
for the songs being short.
I have seen zinnias claim their rights
to speak promises   saying to beholders,
*   "Whatever may be your wish, sir or madam,*
*   I promise you shall have it—today, tomorrow,*
*   somewhere over the blue hills and bright valleys,*
*   it shall be yours to keep—whatever you wish—*
*   we so promise—we zinnias God made for promising."*

I have heard zinnias counseling together:
  "Ever the summer is kind to us,
   summer belonging to us as we belong to summer.
   When God said, 'Let there be summer'
   He also said, 'And let there be zinnias
   bathed in colors called from sunsets and early stars.'
   And God having so spoken
   how can we be either proud or humble?
   how can we be aught else than quiet blooming zinnias?"

   Thus having heard the zinnias
   I shall go again and again to hear the zinnias.

So it was that I grew to regard Connemara and all that
lived on her rolling land and mountainsides in a personal way.
I was devoted to her and felt her promises: delight in the early
morning and in the sun hot on one's back; in the feeling of
power seeing Buppong lift the oaken chair high over his
head and look beyond the pines to the mountains blue in the
distance; in the newborn creatures and generous earth. She
seemed to speak of a faith in the cycles of nature, and in the
infinite capabilities of the human mind and heart.

I once turned to Gramma, in whom I had immense trust,
and asked her how it could ever be bearable to live elsewhere.
She answered that there was a world of beautiful places to
see and live in. I respected her reply, but was more than a
little disbelieving.

Even the remotest corners of Connemara had been made
familiar by the family. There were trails leading through
streams, flanked by mountain laurel and rhododendron that
bloomed each spring as if the festival of the century was upon
us. The family walked long on such mountain paths, and
Buppong and I would bring back to the house stones or nuts
or leaves whose shape or color pleased us, or pieces of wood

that reminded us of some bird in flight or a creature we had once met in a dream.

Returning to Connemara for a summer visit a few years ago, I suddenly realized that there was no art in the Sandburg house except that from the land around us and from the family itself. The paintings in the house were done by my grandmother's brother, Edward Steichen, or my mother or Margaret, and there were a few photographs of Uncle Ed's. And then there were all those pieces of wood gathered on the walks—and the stones, acorns, pine cones and horse chestnuts —each one selected and respected. They seemed in place among the mountains of reading materials stacked about the house and the people who moved throughout it or visited it.

OMA

Knowing just how the blue of her eyes
was struck with sunlight and laughter . . .
Feeling just why the touch of her hands
was born of warm breads and children and roses . . .
Understanding the will and the faith of her ways . . .

I am grateful when she seats herself in this room
she never saw
and speaks to me of daring and dreamers.

—PAULA STEICHEN
Connemara, 1967

Edward Steichen

Oma

These were the people of the past...

There were people at Connemara with whom I never sat down at the breakfast table, and yet I knew just how it was they baked crusty loaves of bread or arranged roses into hats. These were the people of the past—my grandmother's mother and father, my great-great-great grandfather—ancestors through the ages who had some quality about them that made their names come back again and again to the tongues of Connemara folk.

Gradually I had an image of these people, and looking at the pillared white house I could feel that every room was filled. Even when everyone was in town and Connemara was peopleless she never seemed empty—but like a strong gentle creature in the sun and perfectly content.

When I was three my grandfather and Uncle Ed inscribed a copy of *Steichen the Photographer*: "Dear Snick—beloved Karlen Paula—this now your book first belonged to 'Old Oma' as she called herself, your great-grandmother who carried your grand-Uncle Ed in her arms as a baby from the Grand Duchy of Luxemburg to the Port of New York USA and on over the Alleghenies past three of the Great Lakes and on to Hancock, Michigan, where the baby grew and became what you see in this book. Old Oma's husband, as you know, who was your great-grandfather, himself had a great-grandfather, who in Luxemburg was conscripted by Napoleon, made the march to Russia, returning to Luxemburg to eventually die at the age of 106 years. Your grandmother Lilian Paula Elizabeth Ann, University of Chicago Phi Beta Kappa, gave this book to her daughter Helga, your mother. Like your brother John Carl who has a higher number of this book, if and when you read it we believe you will be slightly more interested in both the forms and apparitions of life—Buppong." The inscription continued, in Edward Steichen's handwriting, "and when the Princess Paula carries her little son in her arms over mountains past rivers and lakes will she give him the kiss I gave her today September the seventh nineteen forty six. your Uncle Ed."

Oma became the most familiar of all Connemara's spirits. Often I heard the story of her crossing the Atlantic in the hold of a ship with her eighteen-month-old son, Edward Jean Steichen. Her husband, Jean Pierre, had sailed to America at least a year before, in hopes of finding a fine life for his family. After six months all letters from him had stopped. Finally, his worried wife placed her belongings in a suitcase, wrapped a blanket around her baby boy and sailed for the New York Harbor.

Without knowing her husband's exact address, she travelled across the new land with the baby in her arms—searched for and found her husband in Chicago, sitting in a boardinghouse room, ill and unable to find work. The trunks he had brought with him across the ocean, full of goods and linens for the new home, stood half empty—their contents had been traded for rent. The small inheritance he had carried across the Atlantic with him was gone.

With her family in poor straits, it was the peasant girl, Mary Kemp Steichen, who learned that there was work to be found in the copper mines of Hancock, Michigan, and who settled the family in the neighborhood there. She made friends and, when she saw that the mining was not good for her husband's health, attempted several different businesses, finally establishing a millinery shop.

In 1883, a daughter was born to the Luxemburgers. Her birth name was Lilian Maria; she was baptized Anna Elizabeth, her confirmation name was to become Magdalene, and they nicknamed her with a Luxemburg endearment: Paus'l. Paus'l, or Lily as she was alternately called, grew up wearing beautiful curls and her mother's hats—both to her distress. She was an important model for her mother's goods and the successful shop.

During my years of growing at Connemara, I often listened to Gramma's stories of her youth. I was in awe of Oma's strength and the powerful affection her children felt for her. "Gramma, did Oma have a sense of humor?" I once asked. "Oh, yes!" came the reply. "But more than that, a sense of humanity. She was always doing something for someone. And of course she had a sense of humor!"

I pictured Gramma as a serious child, wheeling her doll carriage in front of the church on one of the few paved walks in town. I was told of the time that Gramma was chosen to present a bouquet to a visiting Bishop, and in her excitement threw the flowers into the old man's face. I heard of the two children baking potatoes with friends in the marsh one summer when Oma returned to Luxemburg for a visit, and about the parrot the Steichen family kept as a pet for several years, who would call out raucously, "Eddy, get up, it's eight o'clock!" Eventually he was sold because of his habit of answering a knock on the door with, "Come in, come in!"—sometimes to the aggravation of the visitor when the family was away and the door was locked.

Best of all I loved the story of Oma's bargain purchase after the family had moved to Milwaukee—of one hundred boxes of red roses with which to decorate her hats. She had bought them as Opa stood by, critical and disbelieving. "You'll never sell all those roses!" The boxes filled a whole room, stacked one on the other—one hundred boxes of roses.

The next Sunday, Lily went to church in a hat of roses, and the women thought, "If the hatmaker's daughter wears roses, roses must be in style." At the shop, Eddy was painting posters of beautiful ladies in hats flowing with roses—and the show windows seemed a garden. Within a month all the roses were gone, and Milwaukee was in style!

Throughout the years of Gramma's youth, Oma gave the two children strong support and had infinite faith in them. Opa was skeptical of the ways of his willful family. He could not understand why his son wanted to waste water in a dark room of chemicals and prints. He could not understand why his daughter longed to go to high school and he refused to allow her to attend.

At seventeen, the boy became an apprentice in a lithographic firm. He was paid a dollar a week the first year, two the next, then three, then four. He was set to learning the intricacies of lettering. It was not until a noon hour, shortly before Christmas, that the owner, Mr. von Cotzhausen, discovered him painting a water color of birds as a present for his mother. He was transferred to the art section then, and in his fourth year his salary soared to twenty-five dollars a week. While he was at the lithographic firm, he formed an Art

Students' League with other young artists—and the group paid for models and spent long hours together. At last, at twenty-one, he concluded his apprenticeship and his years in Milwaukee and sailed for Paris, the art center of the world.

Like her brother, when my grandmother was graduated from the eighth grade, she was expected to learn a trade. Oma hoped her daughter would grow enthusiastic about the millinery business, and she was kept at home for one year. At the end of that time, Lily still longed for more education, and her mother would not force her to stay home. Paus'l knew of a convent in Canada where the mother of her best friend, Phyllis Shultheiss, had gone to school. At sixteen she set out for a year at the convent, where she soon became the best student—taking fourteen and fifteen subjects at a time. She was intensely religious at first. She read St. Augustine, and seeing the nuns remaining at prayer all night, she, too, knelt before the altar from dusk until dawn.

It was during the end of this year at the convent that she read an article by Mark Twain in the *Atlantic Monthly* which told of young girls being forced into prostitution in different countries. She asked herself how there could be a God if such things occurred. Her friend Phyllis was of a Catholic family also, and she was asking similar questions. Mr. Shultheiss sent to Germany for a set of books which would explain the dilemma to these two young doubters. Lily, who had taken logic at the convent among the fifteen other subjects, found a pronouncement on the seventh page which had no logical foundation, and upon which everything else was based. She turned from the Catholic religion.

Oma was greatly distressed and took her to a priest in a large cathedral in Milwaukee. An intelligent man, he listened and reassured Oma that as long as her daughter believed that she was doing right, she was still religious at heart. Nine years later, in a letter to her future husband, Paus'l was to explain, "I am not hostile to theology. I simply have no theology. I recognize a universal religion of humanism and joy-in-life— a religion common to all—to those who accept theologies and to those who have no theologies."

After the decisive year in the convent, she made up her mind to go to college. That summer she taught herself all she would have learned in high school necessary to pass the entrance exams. She studied algebra, geometry, French, German, botany, and read all the books that a former teacher advised her to know. At seventeen she passed the exams and entered the University of Illinois. There she took the required subjects and decided to transfer to the more exciting University of Chicago, where she could study under Thorstein Veblen and Oscar Lovell Triggs. She was thoughtful and intent. She became a vegetarian, eating at the Seventh Day Adventist dining room, and joined the Socialist Club of Chicago.

Although she did not take any part in the "university life" during her college years, she did enjoy the discussions and the intensity at the Socialist headquarters. She had first become interested in the movement years before as she read Shelley— an independent thinker in both political and religious fields. She translated two German books for the Socialist movement.

In 1903, when she was twenty years old, she graduated from the University of Chicago, her brother sending her a great bunch of lilies for the occasion. The officials had asked her for her name, and when she answered "Lilian Steichen," they insisted on a middle name also. She gave it: Lilian Anna Maria Elizabeth Steichen, thoughtfully leaving the Magdalene out.

Four times on the graduation program, two lines were allotted for one graduate:

The degree of Bachelor of Philosophy is conferred by the University upon:

LILIAN ANNA MARIA ELIZABETH STEICHEN

Honors in excellence in particular departments of the Senior Colleges are awarded the following student:

LILIAN ANNA MARIA ELIZABETH STEICHEN   (*English*)

Honorable mention for excellence in the work of the Senior Colleges is awarded the following students . . . [among five others]:

LILIAN ANNA MARIA ELIZABETH STEICHEN

Election to membership in the Beta of Illinois Chapter of Phi Beta Kappa is awarded each of the following students . . . [along with one other student]:

LILIAN ANNA MARIA ELIZABETH STEICHEN

The two Steichen children had grown up with strength and independence. The bond between the two of them and their mother never weakened. My grandfather, who grew to love the three of them deeply, once wrote of their mother-child relationship: "It is a rare thing—so deep and close a chumminess—with such a foundation on the things that are everlasting." He described Oma to his wife-to-be: "[She's] as unique in her way as you. She's Whitmanic. Nothing but the limit, the farthest and highest for her boy and girl. Nothing but the limit for herself, working in the scope of her chances. A rapt enthusiast, giving all, risking all, and no surety of returns."

Gramma recently said to me, "I am nothing of a mystic, but Oma's presence has been in every house I have lived in." Even here at Connemara, a place Oma never set foot on or lived to know of, she has been alive and, now, as when I was a child, I feel I have known the grey-blue of her eyes, the surety of her smiles. There is some part of Oma in words my Uncle Ed wrote to Gramma when he was twenty-two and had just returned to Paris from the Photo Secession Exhibition at Pittsburgh. Gramma was eighteen and had written some poems which Ed had seen. "You have the art and the ability," he wrote to her, ending a letter. "It is merely the fight for the recognizing of it. It will be that always and the greater and better we do, the harder the battle. . . . I myself can hardly make ends meet—but the other thing we live does not fluctuate with Wall Street but within ourselves—be it the belching, bellying roar of Pittsburgh with its wealth and its slavery, with its genius of labor and ignorance—or be it the calm and silence of the snow and moonlight. It lies within *us* the beauty of all these—and it is for *us* to create and give—and it is art. Lovingly—Edward."

My grandmother met Charles August Sandburg in February, 1908, when she was twenty-four years old. After leaving Chicago, she had taught Latin in high school for two years in Valley City, North Dakota, and then for another two years in Princeton, Illinois. She met the young Swede at the Social Democratic Headquarters in Milwaukee. Her parents had moved to a little farm fourteen miles outside of the town, which Ed had bought for them. On this occasion, Gramma was returning from a visit there, on her way back to Princeton —staying in Milwaukee with old friends for just a day or two before catching the train to Illinois.

On the 27th of March that year, Buppong visited Gramma at Oma and Opa's farm for a weekend. It was during those few days that she persuaded him to change his name from Charles to Carl—and that they decided to be married. The

Edward Steichen

Gramma, 1923

two had written to each other almost every· day since they had first met, Buppong declaring, "The coincidence of our ideas and whims and plans is something I would not have believed till—the Wonder Woman came!"

When she declared that she did not have the genius to write poetry as he did, and that he must accept her for what she was, not an illusion, he declared, "I would rather be a poem like you than write poems—I would rather embody the big things as you do than carve or paint or write them—You inspire art—and its living! . . . You're a genius!—Paula—"

The two of them had a love for "The People." What they wanted in the Socialist movement, has, by and large, been accomplished today in Social Security and pension plans, in Medicare and the laws protecting age and working conditions in factories. In the spring of 1908 Buppong wrote to Gramma: "All the big people are simple, as simple as the unexplored wilderness. They love the universal things that are free to everybody. Light and air and food and love and some work are enough. In the varying phases of these cheap and common things, the great lives have found their joy."

These words are in essence what they practiced at Connemara forty and fifty years later. Their home, as I knew it so much later, contained only what was essential and of meaning to those who dwelled inside. My grandmother's bedroom is a lesson in simplicity and loveliness, unequalled in my eyes, except by the open fields and clear skies. The high walls are white, the inexpensive bedspreads are white with small flowers woven into them. The windows are many and curtainless, looking out onto the tops of trees and mountains. It is a spacious room, but holds only two beds, two chairs, an uncluttered dresser, a bureau and a table. There are three photographs in the room taken by Uncle Ed, and I remember that when I was a child the bay windows always held on each ledge a solemn, sweet parade of African violets. And of course there are bookshelves!

When I was seven or eight I used to dance alone in my grandmother's room, singing my own songs and making up my own steps over the carpet of flowers on the floor. I could see a stage of costumed dancers performing alongside me. Though I went through phases in later years when I coveted belongings and could not quite understand my grandmother, in time I appreciated her ways—seeing that it was the mind and spirit that created her surroundings and moods, not the objects about her; understanding her statement, "It is not a gift that always measures how much a person loves."

Gramma was never interested in public attention, and judged the worth of things and people by her own standards. While

Buppong and Uncle Ed, 1923

Edward Steichen

she was pleased about the honors bestowed on her brother and husband over the years, it never changed her interests or way of life. She is as much a liberal at eighty-five as she was at twenty-five. She can still hike five miles and rise rested the next day after six hours of sleep. She eats as simply now as she did before she was married, when she would write of having had a dinner of two eggs and an apple or fresh pineapple and a slice of bread.

Before the eventual serenity and comfort of Connemara, the Sandburgs had years of uncertainty, wondering how the next rent bill would be paid, and there were domestic tragedies. The first baby, my Aunt Margaret, was stricken with epilepsy; the second, another girl, died at birth; and the third, my Aunt Janet, never grew to be capable of independence from the home. Yet the fourth child, Helga, was normal, and the three girls remember their childhood together as a sunny time. The Sandburgs had a way of keeping hold of optimism and a strong acceptance of reality. In an early letter to Buppong, young Paus'l Steichen had said, "I have a way of comparing frescoed ceilings with the sky set with stars—Orion and the rest—that always nips in the bud any possible infringement on my part of the tenth commandment 'thou shalt not covet thy neighbor's goods!' The sky is the big arched ceiling— the only one in the world big enough for *us* anyway—the sky is the really beautiful ceiling that is ours for the looking, since we have eyes that see. . . . With such eyes as we have, our only difficulty will be not being able to enter into possession of all the things that *are* really ours—ours for the mere looking—We won't have time enough to walk over all the land we really own (because we have power to appreciate it!)—we won't have time to walk to the ends of our domain. . . ."

That was the philosophy that overshadowed everything else. It was revealed to me in its essence one day when I was nine and was worried over the fact of death. "Gramma," I asked, "what would you do if all of us died? Could you go on living?" Her reply was unforgettable. "As long as I have the earth and the sky I can live forever."

"ARRIVING USUAL TRAIN THURSDAY MORNING
HOORAY HOORAY HOORAY—NO SIG"

—EDWARD STEICHEN
Telegram, 1949

Buppong and Uncle Ed, 1949

There were visitors...

My grandmother's brother, Edward Steichen, was known to me as "Uncle Ed." Though I was aware that he had made the photographs that hung about the house, and though I was told that the young, strikingly handsome man who looked down at me through one large frame was my friend in days before I was born, when he was just taking hold of the world— the reality of Uncle Ed, in my childhood, was in his happiest of eyes and laughter and his wonderfully mysterious ways. He came occasionally from his faraway home, and when he went away he left behind a family in love. Perhaps that is why his visits seemed so touched with magic. The excitement over his coming built up like electricity in the house, and when he arrived it was a festival of gaiety and celebration.

His voice was as resonant and unforgettable as his laughter, and his silences were punctuated with giggles as we children followed him on tiptoes throughout the house—bent on some bit of mischief. Coming into the hall one afternoon, the family found John Carl and him taking the doors off their hinges, John full of glee at this unprecedented act and Uncle Ed with a simple explanation, "If you don't take doors off their hinges, how are you going to know how to put doors back on their hinges?"

In the basement at Connemara was a mammoth furnace, which had to be stoked with coal each morning by the caretaker. We told Uncle Ed of the caretaker's misfortune when he went to stoke the furnace after one of our Siamese cats had moved her growing litter of kittens into the furnace room. Sa-wang had attacked the unknowing man, leaping onto his back and leaving long claw marks across his shoulders. We solemnly led Uncle Ed to the furnace room to show him the spot of ambush.

The next afternoon with innocent excitement he rushed in to tell us that he had just been to the moon and back in the spaceship that he and John and Buppong had been nailing together. As proof of his journey he held out his hands filled with cinders taken from the moon's craters. Believing he was capable of anything, it was days before we wide-eyed children realized that the cinders had been brought up from the furnace room in the basement.

From the day that "Eddy" had met my grandfather, on his first visit to Oma and Opa's farm, their friendship had grown steadily. Buppong wrote to Gramma, after seeing photos taken at their first meeting, "Edward Steichen is an artist. We all know our best selves, the selves we love. And he caught a self I pray to be all the time. By what wizardry of insight and penetration he came to get that phase of me in so little a time, I don't know. It took more than eyes—it took heart and soul back of the eyes." From New York Uncle Ed wrote his opinion of the marriage between his little sister and a man he had met only once. "I have that peculiar feeling that I sometimes get about such things—sort of a premonition that it will be great."

Uncle Ed

By the time I was born, Sandburg had published a biography of the photographer, *Steichen the Photographer,* and Steichen had taken numerous photographs of the poet. They had collaborated on *The Road to Victory* exhibition and each was deeply interested in the other's thoughts and works.

Together they would tell wonderful tales to John Carl and me, emphasizing a turn in the story with widened eyes and dramatic motions of the arms; or they simply shouted back and forth to one another and shook their fists with imaginary

141

Uncle Ed testing the validity of one of John's magic tricks

fury until the family was sliding off their chairs in laughter. Once Helga organized a horse show in the orchard in honor of Uncle Ed's arrival. It consisted of three saddle horses, one pony and the work team, and a hand-wound victrola which ground out Sousa's March under the apple trees. Occasionally, the two men and we children would put on living-room programs for the family—songs and a demonstration of John's latest invention and a dramatic recitation of poetry by Uncle Ed. If John gave a magic show in our production, Uncle Ed was always chosen to test the reality of the magician's powers. If he was asked to prove that a coin was not a fake, he would bite on it with grimaces and gnashing of teeth before announcing at last that it *was* authentic. Whatever you asked of Uncle Ed, he did it well!

My earliest recollection of this treasured visitor is of his voice calling me "Princess Paula" and "Paus'l the Second," and the sight of his shining blue eyes and his face made of smiles. On the front lawn he would swing me round and round by his arms until the two towering pink dogwood trees above us were a dream of spinning blossoms and the dogs were barking wildly at our side.

Always when Uncle Ed was at Connemara, I would turn to bed unwilling but exhausted. In the morning the family room would be strewn with the glasses and ashtrays of the late previous night. At my grandfather's place would be a pair of dice he had fashioned from a piece of bread, numbered with fork-prong marks. John and I could sense that the room

Buppong providing music for a living-room puppet show

had only been emptied a few hours before, and we wondered at the time these grownups spent together and the words that they exchanged.

There was one summer night we were allowed to stay awake into the darkness. Out on the rock behind the house—the sheet of granite stretching flat three hundred feet, and then turning down the hillside to the lake—Uncle Ed gave a party. A fire was set ablaze and a parade of visiting relatives and Connemara folk marched and ran back and forth between the white house and the rock, carrying huge crockery pots of potato salad, and meats to be cooked on the fire, and dishes and goat milk and fresh vegetables, and marshmallows for the children.

Uncle Ed knew many of our songs, and sometimes, from him, I caught a rare sense of time. By the firelight I watched him and my grandparents, my aunts and Helga suddenly singing with surety and a passionate sweetness a song I had never heard before—a song forgotten at Connemara—from the days and the visits on the dunelands in Michigan or even before that—in Elmhurst, Illinois. On into the dark the family would sing—such a clear sky overhead! Lying on my back on the granite I could see how the pine tops mixed with the stars and felt that the night was filled with music.

There was no declaration of an end to the party; the tunes decided for us. Suddenly "Tipperary" was over and "Bye Bye Blackbird" came, and then "There's a Long Long Trail A-Winding," and finally "Good Night, Ladies." Almost asleep, I was given a parcel to carry back to the house, and then the adults put out the fire and gathered the papers and stray marshmallow sticks.

The next morning Uncle Ed left for his home in Connecticut, and for a long time afterward members of the family would catch themselves smiling at some memory of his visit, and wishing that his next visit were to be tomorrow.

Though no other guest could compare with Uncle Ed, another man who distinguished himself with John Carl and me was Ed Murrow, whose friendly crew of television men visited us for two weeks at the end of one summer. We liked and respected Mr. Murrow, with his good-humored patience, deep-throated laughter, awesome height and continual smoking. John Carl spent days with his sound men, taping crickets and frogs in the evenings and the songs of birds at dawn.

I appointed myself guide of the barns and pastures and was eager to show off my pets among the herd to Mr. Murrow and his associates. I recall vividly one disastrous filming, when I was to lead the goats up the lane from pasture to their evening milking. Such a thing cannot be contrived, since the goats know exactly what time of day they can expect to be milked and fed, so at the proper hour the cameras were rolling and the sound equipment was set up. I brought the goats up the lane as scheduled, but, for some reason, instead of playing my part as goatherd, I led my pet, Bebe, the prettiest of all, directly into the camera—ruining the entire take as the goats scattered past into the barnyard and I stood pointing out to the cameraman the unique markings of Bebe. I only remember him saying, "Good God, no!"

Adlai Stevenson visited one spring, too, and I was his staunch supporter for all the years to come. He was beloved by the family—even by Ella, who went to the polls for the first time in her life the year she voted for him. There were other guests—men from Washington, old friends from Chicago, occasionally a celebrity from California—but I remember only a few with clarity. There were also numerous, brief visitors who were not family or friends, but photographers

145

or reporters whom Buppong liked to see sometimes, remembering his own newspaper days. And then there was often an afternoon visit from a desperate student or writer who wanted some quick equations for success. Occasionally Buppong would turn these people away if he was deep at work, explaining to them that if he spent all his time talking, he would never have time to write. But often he would listen and give a few words of encouragement to the more earnest, serious ones. Early I learned from him to be wary of students who did not want to search out the answers they could have found in books, and of writers who did not have enough insight and pride to evaluate and market their works without the help of an established author.

Letters sometimes preceded the visitors or hopeful interviewers. At times Buppong set them aside, labelled "for Paula and John." On one paper we would see a request: "The most authoritative source of information about a person, I am told, is that which comes directly from him. Consequently, I am writing to ask you about yourself and your literary works. I should like to come to your study for an informal interview with you. Would Feb. 24*th* or Feb. 25*th* from four to four-thirty o'clock be convenient? Thank you." At the bottom of the page would be Buppong's note to his grandchildren: "In the case of an author of 16 books, she might try reading some of the books, leaving him more time for his own thoughts. . . ."

Once in a while a letter would show a glimmer of understanding. A young boy closed his extensive list of questions with the line, "If this is too much trouble don't waste much time on me." This prompted Buppong to note for John Carl and me with a smile, "This last thought is keen tho abrupt— CS." Most of these kinds of letters were never answered. Buppong would declare, "I'm not running for public office, and a man has to decide what is important in life." But sometimes he would send off a reply, "My only advice to you is to beware of advice and to be never afraid of toil, solitude or prayer."

Of course, there were letters that made no demands, simply thanking Buppong for the words or thoughts within a book. These were sweet to receive and when he had time he would answer them. "Your letter is one to treasure. You cover much ground in it and the least I can say is that your words make me feel less useless in this age of chaos. May luck stars be over you."

Helga, who helped her father with his paper work, recalls in one of her journals that the poet sometimes regarded a box or drawer stuffed full with envelopes, and declared, "I guess I'll clean this out. There are some letters there that I ought to answer. But the trouble is some of these people may have moved. . . ."

"Dear Buppong
I will be glad
when you
come home.
I saw a seal a
clown and a
horse at
the circus.
I like school.
I love you
mister.
Paula"

"Dear dear Paula Snick   Your letter ending 'I love you
mister' is here next to my heart and what I say is I love
you five six and I love you a thousand and then ten
million—

your old times
Buppong"

DEAR BUPPONG
PWILL BE GLAD
WHEN YOU
COME HOME
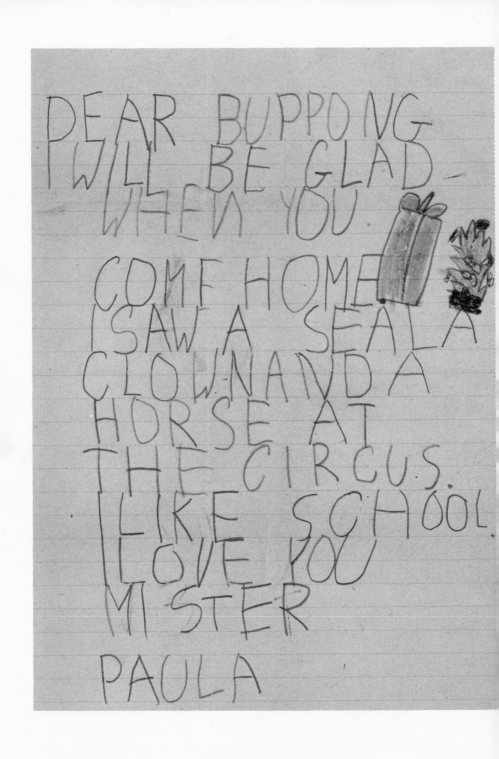
ISAW A SEAL A
CLOWN AND A
HORSE AT
THE CIRCUS.
I LIKE SCHOOL.
I LOVE YOU
MISTER
PAULA

Dear dear Paula Snick   Your letter
ending "I love you mister" is here next to
my heart and what I say is I love you five
six and I love you a thousand and then
ten million =

                    your old times
                            Buppong

Dana Steichen

Snick

School and...advice over the years...

When I was six years old, I joined John Carl at Rosa Edwards Elementary School in Hendersonville. Each morning and afternoon Helga drove us the five-mile route to and from school. It became our custom to recite lessons, especially the multiplication tables, and to sing songs during these rides. My favorite tunes were always the ballads of the West and of cowboys, but we learned "Old Dan Tucker," "Barbra Allen" and "Old Black Joe," too, and we made up our own version of "Tipperary," which ran:

> It's a short way to Connemara,
> It's a short way to go.
> It's a short way to Connemara
> And the sweetest goats we know.
> Goodby, County Court House!
> Farewell, Hatch's Feed Store
> It's a short, short way to Connemara
> And our heart's right there!

The beginning of school marked a twenty-five-mile trip to Asheville with Helga, where we children saw department stores which were equipped with elevators and seemed gigantic— filled with an unfamiliar musty scent. There we excitedly tried on the clothes Helga selected for us to wear on special occasions and to school in the winter months.

The yearly trip to Asheville was the extent of my travelling until I was ten years old and moved from Connemara. My view of the world before that was a simple one. I wrote of it when I was seven: "I am a little girl. My name is Karlen Paula. We have a farm. We have goats. We make our living on goats. Do you like and have goats?"

Though I was used to the expanses of Connemara, the new and unfamiliar school seemed huge to me and filled with mysteries. I never lost a fear of crossing through the dim basement from the cafeteria to the playground during the lunch period. When I was in second grade and being outfitted for my part in *Hansel and Gretel,* I was filled with excitement as I saw the dusty trunks full of costumes being brought from storage. I hoped desperately that some day I would be able to explore all the closed doors and locked trunks in the building.

Helga had taught John Carl and me to read and write and do simple arithmetic before we started grammar school. As is true with most children, I learned more from my family than I did from the classroom—and yet I liked school very much, and found there, for the first time, playmates of my own age.

My memories of Rosa Edwards are limited: the only one of first grade is of being spanked one day for something I didn't do; and the most vivid memory from third grade is of the day when it was discovered that no one in the room, including me, could write his ABC's on the blackboard without a mistake. I came closest, as I recall, having had the benefit of my Aunt Janet's teaching of the song which ends ". . . now you have my ABC's, what do you think of me?" But I had never quite mastered the proper sequence of the S-T-U-V section.

That year, too, I was elected president of the joint assembly of third and fourth grades—and remember distinctly wanting to be secretary of the grades, and being very disappointed when I learned I was president. We candidates campaigned from classroom to classroom giving speeches, and, no doubt, my playful exchanges with Buppong had prepared me for such speechmaking just as it had for the role of Gretel the year before.

Second grade was my favorite of the three years at Rosa Edwards. The teacher, Mrs. Sossoman, had filled the room with plants, and with cages and aquariums holding growing pollywogs, small reptiles, cocoons and chrysalises. We painted and drew a great deal that winter and were photographed surrounding the cans of food and fruit and clothing we had collected for poor families at Christmas.

It was the next year, while I was in third grade, that I first experienced the reaction of an appreciative public to my grandfather. In the spring of the year the school asked Buppong to give a reading of *Rootabaga Stories* to an assembly of students. As president of the intermediate grades I was to introduce my grandfather after conducting class business, and present a bunch of roses to him after his reading. I had never been to a lecture of any kind and the attitude of the adults toward the speaker astonished me. My poise left me completely, the *Rootabaga Stories* seemed utter foolishness, and in my embarrassment and confusion I refused to present the bunch of roses to the speaker.

There was one more public performance, shortly after the first one at the grade school, in which I figured with as little grace. In a large hall in a nearby summer park, the family went to hear Buppong give a program of poems and songs. Toward the end he asked John Carl and me to come onto the stage to sing with him. We went, solemnly separating from each other, as was our natural tendency, and walking toward our grandfather from opposite ends of the stage. I recall a lonely realization that one could barely see the hundreds of faces beyond the floodlights. I noticed that from my knee was trailing a long piece of gauze bandage which had been taped there to cover a wide bruise from a slide down one of Connemara's rocky slopes. I do not recall how well I sang, or whether I sang at all. I only remember the applause as I walked across the stage trailing the loosened gauze, and my certainty that the audience did not really want to hear me sing, but was simply being respectful to my grandfather.

Those were my only performances alongside Buppong in the early years. I felt easier with my grandfather as a companion walking up the broad path to the top of Little Glassy, pausing to note the bluets in our way and the foxgloves growing wild at the granite base. On such walks we could laugh at his name for the small mountain's rocky slope, "Precipitous Declivity." We shared secrets there in the wilderness of the hills, and I could always trust my grandfather to keep them.

Buppong recorded some dialogue from one of our walks up Little Glassy, typing in his shorthand fashion on a yellow sheet of paper:

"Snick after looking at Rock Spring Cave, 'Buppong it's mysterious. Y must cm nd see it Bpng, it's mysterious.' She leads: 'I hav t go ahead nd opn th gate nd do everything special' . . . w wondrfl scorn 'Wd y like to live in a town hse? Nothin t look at—just go out a-visiting!' . . . on finding cave 'If y really look arnd in the forest y'll find it's better tn a house. . . . Th moss here is so beautiful y cn hardly stnd it.' Nearing top of rock I mention th sunset circling sky nd 'Th sunset is everywhr ts evening!" nd Snick, 'I feel like I'm surrounded w th world don't you?' "

Buppong was unassuming and we children appreciated this without defining it. He would laugh with the family at the continued popularity of his little poem, "Fog," reciting it in a different version, "De fog come on itti bitti kitti footsies. He sit down on Chicago an—whamo—he gone—" He was patient with us, amused—taking a central interest in our learning, and giving me a deep love for fantasy and language. From 1948 I have one of his familiar tales which he typed, entitling and explaining it as follows: "THE MYSTERY OF TONGUES, A Fabular Narrative written by the Author CARL SANDBURG for his Beloved and Distinctive Granddaughter KARLEN PAULA and Intended for Instruction and Practice in Better Pronunciation of Vowels and Consonants employed in Common Speech and Having further Intentions as an Imaginary Incident subsequent to the Abandonment of the famous Construction Job known in History as the Tower of Babel and preceding the Difficulties Familiar to the Official Translators of the United Nations Anno Domini 1948."

It is a somewhat moral tale about three "boobledoobers," Oochmah Oochmah, Plunka Plunka and Hubba Hubba, each whose own name comes from his lips as easily as "a fish, a pickled fish in a dish," but who had great difficulty pronouncing the names of the others (". . . it squeezed their mouths and it pushed and pulled their tongues up and under in a twist. And the faces they made were fish faces and dish faces . . ."). Not one of the boobledoobers wants to drop his own identity and become like the other, and none of them do; but they finally go their separate ways remembering the farewell words of Oochmah Oochmah: "When summer comes and winter goes and time passes and the years chase us hither and yon and we grow older because we cannot again be younger, let us not forget we are all boobledoobers, born and made to be boobledoobers—and not one of us can run away from it. . . . I am bidding you good-by now and telling you be plunka plunka and be hubba hubba but remember sometimes your little friend who must be oochmah oochmah."

Words did not always have to be in the form of such fantastic names in order to roll and twist in our mouths. My grandfather loved Indian words, and the simple names of simple people, and a city's rolling title: "Neworleeeeens." The enjoyment of words was in every sentence he spoke or wrote throughout his life. A 1949 inscription in my *Lincoln Collector* reads just as Buppong often spoke, "For Missy and Snick and Karlen Paula with love taller than the Smokies and Mount Mitchell and deeper than the Atlantic and mysterious as the archipelagoes of Oceanica."

Equalling this love of language was Buppong's reverence for nature. Though most of what I learned from him was in our walks and talks, occasionally he gave me an open-sided envelope with a message on the outside, such as the one reading, "Snick—all the four seasons of the year are good. Here a Japanese lady tells you why she finds them good. Buppong." Inside was a leaf from "the Notebook of Carl Sandburg—Sat June 11 1927." He had written: "Little Japanese prints made of words are found in the 'Pillow Sketches' of our Japanese lady of the year 1000 A.D., Sei Shonagon. On a silk paper used for pillows, she wrote of the four seasons of the year. And the seasons she knew then in 1000 A.D. were much like the seasons known now:

'In spring, I love to watch the dawn grow gradually whiter and whiter, till a faint rosy tinge crowns the mountain's crest, while slender streaks of purple cloud extend themselves above.

'In summer, I love the night, not only when the moon is shining, but the dark too, when the fireflies cross each other's paths in their flight, or when the rain is falling.

'In autumn, it is the beauty of the evening which most deeply moves me as I watch the crows seeking their roosting places in twos and threes and fours, while the setting sun sends forth his beams gorgeously as he draws near the mountain's rim. Still more is it delightful to see the lines of wild geese pass, looking exceedingly small in the distance. And when the sun has quite gone down, how moving it is to hear the chirruping of insects or the sighing of the wind!

'In winter, how unspeakably beautiful is the snow: But I also love the dazzling whiteness of the hoar frost and the intense cold even at other times. Then it is meet quickly to fetch charcoal and kindly fires. And let not the gentle warmth of noon persuade us to allow the embers of the hearth or the brazier to become a white heap of ashes!'

"She loved life and could tell about it—this lady."

Through the years Buppong continued to pass on pieces of writing and pictures which he thought would be of benefit. "Dear Snick and Johannas—Here are portraits of people who lived 200 and 300 years ago. You should be pleased to look at them, study about them, and again look and see. To see is more important than to look. So says your undersubscribed grandfather—Buppong 1951 Anno Domini." In the envelope were portraits painted by Shelley, Hilliard, Crosse, Rochard, Lens and Cosway, extracted from a *Coronet* magazine of 1937. He had penned a title for the group on the outside envelope: "A Little Album of Vanished Ladies, Boy with Violin and Boy in Rags."

At a time when he was rereading Shakespeare, Buppong sent the following pieces of useful advice to his granddaughter, who had recently moved to Virginia:

Dear Snick

As you well know there is a widespread custom of one person saying to another, "Oh, shut up!" and the answer coming swiftly and immediately, "Oh, shut up yourself!" Now I find in Shakespeare's time it was done differently. Instead of "Oh, shut up!" it was "CHARM YOUR TONGUE!" to which came the response, "I WILL BE LIBERAL AS THE AIR IN MY SPEECH!" Now I have seen you often having not merely perfect but exquisite manners and I call your attention to the foregoing technique in behavior for whatever it may be worth to you and your studious lovable carrot-haired brother for whatever it may be worth to you and to him. Tall elegant bushels of love to the both of you. I think of you as my Mexican Zinnia. Others may have Mexicale Rose but you came in Zinnia time and I see three of them before me now, thoughtful in a quiet dreaminess. So I say Pax Vobiscum and Yours Forever

Buppong

My dear Snick

You have on occasion a vehement, picturesque and eloquent flow of speech. I suspect that Shakespeare must have known some young lady somewhat like yourself who as a rebuff to one who had spoken a vile slander, let fly the three words:

"Filth, thou liest!"

I send this to you as merely the impression of a moment and a small oddity that might interest you and to say again pax vobiscum and may the good Lord guide your footsteps in righteous paths and may you often, if not ever, do what your deepest clean heart tells you to do.

Buppong

Buppong's advice ranged wide over the years. There was a brief, whimsical early warning put into a book of mine, "Be good and you will be lonesome." And there was a poem he labelled "Advice To a Ten Year Old Granddaughter," which came to me on my birthday in 1953, echoing the counsel he had given me during the years at Connemara:

Stand in the sun and tell your shadow,
"You have never failed me."

Begin with zero, with naught, with nothing:
then count ten and find the numbers the same,
all here the same as yesterday.

Look where anger has spilled blood,
then consult all your angers A to Z.

Study the wingbone of a dry dead bird—
how light it was for flying!

Look easy at the knee-joint of a goat skeleton—
how it could summon a leap from rock to rock!

Contemplate a rose gone to ashes—
the perfect dignity of ashes!

    Make finger motions matching
    a soft wind in high treetops,
Call off the names of fishes and birds you know—
    for the feel of their fins and wings.

Shut your eyes and open windows
on all places and faces you have seen
               worth remembering.

Examine the eight knuckles
of the fingers of your right hand
and the one knuckle of the thumb—
then speak a thank-you to each knuckle
helping every other knuckle.

When a gold half-moon scuds
from behind one silver cloud to hide behind another
it is proper for you to whisper,
"You scud and I scud—from moment to moment
we both scud."

Looking at any big tree with branches spread wide
you may say, "I honor, Oh Tree,
I honor the deep roots unseen underground
holding you seen overground."

If your ears for one fleeting moment
catch the flutter of archangel wings,
speak, saying, "Please remember me!"

In the winter of 1961 I received a letter from Buppong asking me to send him several of my poems. He first acknowledged them on a slip of blue paper on which he had written with one of his stub pencils in large letters, "You're on the beam, I love you and your goddam lovely poems." And shortly afterward it was followed by a serious letter in which he gave advice and closed once again with the phrase he had written so frequently all through the years:

Beloved Snick—

Yeah—write many poems. Write 'em when you have the feeling or when you don't give a good goddam whether the feeling is there. I don't love you for what you have been (1) nor for what you are (2) nor for what you are going to be (3) but for all three of the aforementioned bigod.

Ever yours,
Buppong

My little exiles   the banished ones
the heart keeps turning to them
memory will not be still
remembering how and what they were
the faces and words of them—
hope works on how and where they are—
how they laughed and ran and slept—
their utterly reckless singing gayety—
their perfections of grace and manner—
their ease and quiet at going lonely—
to each of you I say across empty miles
     "whither goest thou little pilgrim?
          do you sometimes remember Gramma and Buppong?"

—CARL SANDBURG
Connemara, 1952

Leaving Connemara...

The morning of Helga's second marriage was an unusually cold one, and the water pipes froze in the basement. As the flowers and champagne were delivered to Connemara by the Hendersonville merchants, the bride could be seen going in and out of the basement doors in blue jeans and a heavy coat —a blowtorch swinging from her hand. We two children watched Helga intently, faces uplifted, as she applied the hot flame to the frozen pipes.

By afternoon the pipes were thawed, the champagne had been cooled 'outside, the carnations and roses were arranged in vases throughout the house, guests began to arrive and I was dressed in a new pink dress and black patent shoes. I was wary of the wedding. Distrustful of a new name for Helga and us children, I had resisted temporarily. "You'all can change if you want to—but I'm going to keep my old name!" Never had I seen so many visitors at Connemara. Helga appeared, regal, in a dress of green velvet, and I fell briefly in love with the bridegroom's brother when he declared he wanted to marry me dressed as I was and carrying a bouquet of carnations.

Then, in June of 1952, Helga, John Carl and I were driving to a new home in Falls Church, Virginia, which our step-father had just acquired. We were leaving Connemara behind —travelling the distance in a blue Ford with Lief and the un-sold remainder of Helga's Siamese cattery in the back seat. I had never known or even visited any other country or home except Connemara, and I resisted the move as I had the new name. Helga was clear, however: "You can stay if you want, but John and I are going."

The afternoon before leaving I went to the barn for a last farewell to the animals and to the pastures already standing rich in the sun of early summer. My favorite, Bebe, blew gently onto my neck as I knelt by the low stone wall on which we had lingered so many evenings after the milking, and buried a treasure of cereal-box rings, colorful stones taken from my old Western belt and holster, a few bright buttons from my grandmother's sewing box and a horseshoe of Re-member's.

The house that we had moved to was a new one in one of the growing suburbs outside Washington, D.C. Our small development was surrounded by pastureland when we first arrived, but during the next eight years we were to witness the disappearance of all the open land about us as ever smaller houses, and finally, high-rise apartments, took the place of the country. I was to spend many nights in the coming years dreaming of ways to sabotage the bulldozers and the real-estate men who tore apart the familiar paths, burned the trees and replaced it all with regular stretches of concrete and row upon row of identical buildings.

I became friends with the few remaining horse owners nearby, these people kindly letting me use their animals, tack and fields at will. Soon I was entertaining automobile drivers by galloping down the super highways bareback with only a piece of rope around the horse's nose, and often I appeared in our quarter-acre back yard with burlap sacks full of manure slung over the back of one of the horses—for Helga's new hedge or garden—the one gift she asked of me.

Helga planted a little forest of twelve trees on the small portion of land where the top soil had been scraped off by the bulldozers and needed constant attention. She grew tomatoes next to the house, and her grafted apple tree beside the bird feeder bore five kinds of apples. At the front of the house she set out a row of privet which grew until we were almost removed from our neighbors.

She approved when I spent long hours in the basement putting saddle soap on the tack my grandmother had shipped to me from Connemara. She listened to me speak of the jumping fields I had set up, and of the strawberry patches I had found in a pasture; and she watched from the kitchen window as I arrived on Chico, the grey horse I rode most often—cantering across the highway and hitching him to an old fence post next to the back yard.

It was at that window that she saw me one day slap Chico repeatedly, impulsively, punishing him for having pulled his reins loose from the post to wander about the adjoining land cropping grass. Helga called me to the kitchen and gave me the most well-remembered reprimand of all those years. "Don't let me ever again see you punish an animal because of your impatience. If a creature disobeys you, it is either through his ignorance that he does so, or your inability to train him." I recalled the photographs of Helga when she was in her teens in Michigan, surrounded by the animals she had trained: her dogs perching in trees, pulling sleds, even riding her horses with the reins held gently between their teeth; her horses bowing, rearing, pulling, kneeling, lying down, standing—all at her quiet command. I listened to her and remembered.

167

During those days when the circus arrived in Falls Church it would put up its tents on an open lot near Seven Corners where a Howard Johnson's now stands. For several years, when it came regularly, John and I would wake before dawn to go to the grounds and get to know the hands and the animals. John would carry water from a stream to the elephants and I usually got a job with the horses. Finding them loose one early morning, I had caught them as I used to catch Pearl and Major many times at Connemara, and had early gained the trust of the circus people.

John Carl and I became somewhat accustomed to the suburban life. The changing of the landscape never seemed to cease and by the time we left, moving to Washington after eight years, the capital city, with its activity and white monuments, seemed more attractive than the overgrown suburbia. Shortly after our departure the last of the pastureland and horses disappeared.

Throughout these years John and I had gone to Connemara often to spend the summer months or for short winter visits. We would board one of the Pullman cars that Buppong had described to us years before, and watch the land spin away before our eyes as the miles to the farm dwindled. We explored the trains from end to end, bracing ourselves as we reeled through the cars. The porters and engineers took an interest in two children travelling alone, and we spent as much time in their private quarters as in the passenger cars. If it was early morning when the train passed "Old Faithful," the great geyser of steam shooting high into the grey and waking dawn, the porters would be sure to rouse John Carl and me so we would not miss the sight.

When the engine pulled into Asheville, Gramma, Buppong and Marne would be assembled on the platform and, if it was summertime, the many mimosas in the city would be in bloom.

Revisiting Connemara, summer 1953

Be jungle dark in your heart
and then find the black moonlight
of a silence holding your soft voice:
"Sleep and peace always wash my heart."

—CARL SANDBURG
fragment of a poem
to Paula Steichen
Connemara, 1953

Geoffrey Gund

One of the Magnolia grandiflora *blossoms*

My last visit to Connemara...

My last visit to Connemara began in the early part of July, 1967. I came with plans to stay for several months, hoping to write about Connemara while I could still walk her paths—sensing that the family could not stay here forever. It was evening when I arrived, and Gramma took me into her spacious white room where my grandfather had slept for the past months. I saw, as quickly as I stepped past the door, that Buppong was changed and ill. I had never known him in his youth or even in his middle years, but this was the first time that I had ever seen him as an old man. Age had swept over him so completely that little more than a shadow was left.

Past the bay window I could see the *Magnolia grandiflora* tree in full blossom. The nurse had put a record on the phono-graph—Chopin—and had set a vase on the table which held one of the magnolia blooms, its petals spread at least a foot wide in architectural loveliness. The blossom's lemon scent filled the room, and I thought of the calls and the secrets that its parent tree had heard those years when John and I swung among the branches with abandon. I thought of Buppong's laughter as he watched his two ragged grandchildren climbing the stairs after an afternoon high in the magnolia. It was the memory of his laughter that would come back again and again through the next weeks before he died. Laughter and songs.

There were moments in the interval when he would step out of the shadow and suddenly become Buppong again. One day I walked into his room wearing a green Mexican dress and his exclamation came quick: "What have we here? I like your dress, Snick, and the color of your hair . . . and the way you walk . . . you know where you're going!"

At midnight before the twenty-second of the month he looked into my grandmother's grey-blue eyes, as he had looked into them sixty years earlier, and said simply the name of the woman he loved, "Paula." The next morning he "breathed away" into death and my grandmother stated quietly to the telephoning press, "Now Carl belongs to the ages."

The funeral took place at the tiny St. John in the Wilderness Episcopal Church with an ease he had requested. A young Unitarian minister blended his own sensitive words sparingly between the poetry of Walt Whitman and of my grandfather. The organist played "John Brown's Body" and "Shout All Over God's Heaven" as Buppong had asked in his poem "Finish," and we tolled the bell once. Uncle Ed entered the chapel white-haired and with a heavy cane, carrying a green bough of pine, broken from one of the front drive's towering sentinel trees. This he laid with dramatic tenderness on his brother-in-law's coffin.

At home the house filled with flowers and telegrams which we placed throughout the house—and I remembered Tallulah Bankhead's deep-throated words over the phone the night before, "It must look like a gangster's funeral with all those flowers!" Buppong would have liked her rolling declaration.

For people who lived away from Connemara, who had known Buppong and his works, it might have been harder to see him die than it was for his family. Realizing only that they had lost a singer of songs, a friend, a man whose works gave something to their lives—death came suddenly and seemed a tragedy. Letters came to console my grandmother, but there were no tears from the white-haired small woman who had often called her husband "Buddy." Gramma asked us, "Why should I mourn Carl's going? Being ill was no way for a man like that to live. His life was full and long, and in the pages of his books I still have much of Carl as he was when he was living and well—not suffering."

In September, with the warning fall winds already on their way, my grandmother, wearing the same low shoes she had worn to the funeral in July, walked with me through streams and over fallen trees on the low side of Glassy Mountain as we followed the boundary fence line for unblazed miles. Wisps of her snow-white hair came loose from their pins—giving her the same independent look she had in a photo her brother had taken in 1900. "Don't forget, Gramma, at any point we've only gone halfway!" I cautioned her occasionally. "I should do this more often!" was her reply. "Now, let's count the fence posts so we can estimate how far this side of the boundary stretches. . . ." Returning to the house hours later, I retired to my room for a late nap, while Gramma, as she was accustomed, went to her desk in the Farm Office to work until midnight.

A month later, she climbed Big Glassy with the family and visitors, her eighty-four-year-old figure walking steadily the three miles over rocks and up the sometimes gutted paths. She talked continually on her way, her familiar light laughter punctuating sentences. When we came to the height, with its view reaching past Hendersonville and the county around, far out to the blue hills of the Smokies, she swept the scene with a motion of her arm and spoke once more of our "million acres of sky." I was reminded of what she wrote to the young Charles Sandburg so many years before: "The sky is the really beautiful ceiling that is ours for the looking, since we have eyes that can see. With such eyes as we have, our only difficulty will be not being able to enter into possession of all the things that *are* really ours—ours for the mere looking. . . . We won't have time to walk to the ends of our domain." And Buppong's reply, "All the big people are simple, as simple as the unexplored wilderness. They love the universal things that are free to everybody. Light and air and food and love and some work are enough. In the varying phases of these cheap and common things, the great lives have found their joy."